Praise for *A Spiritual Path to a Healthy Relationship*

"With rigorously honest good humor, Angie and Steve McCord have let us in on the intimate process of surrendering to love and learning how to give it in the way our partners need. Any recovering person co___ __efit from the deep insights gleaned from these pages. A loving rea___ ____ _le experience."

Judi Hollis, PhD
Creator of the nation's f_____
Author of *Fat Is a Family _____ _____ ____ _eavy,*
and *F_____*

"Steve and Angie have written an _____g, honest, and practical book based in the 'experience, strength, an_ _ope' they have gained in their life together. For singles hoping to find a partner, for those wounded by too many relationships gone awry, or for couples looking to develop deeper and healthier relationships, this book will provide insight and many opportunities to learn. The voice of Angie and Steve, the prayer and the exercises that conclude many chapters, provide not only wisdom but a path to action."

Mary Cross, PhD

• • •

"I would recommend this wonderful book for any two partners who are setting out on this great journey of healing and recovery and want to learn how to do it together."

Peter K Canavan
Licensed Marriage and Family Therapist
Certified Imago Relationship Therapist

• • •

"Longing for a fulfilling romantic partnership leaves us famished for true success stories. I deeply appreciate Steve and Angie's revelations of the specific practices that helped them to evolve as individuals. This practical book demonstrates how a fierce commitment to our own personal growth readies us for a delightful, life-enhancing relationship to unfold."

Linda Bloom
Co-author of *101 Things I Wish I Knew When I Got Married:
Simple Lessons to Make Love Last* and *Secrets of Great Marriages:
Real Truths from Real Couples about Lasting Love*

A SPIRITUAL PATH
TO A
HEALTHY
RELATIONSHIP

A Spiritual Path

TO A

Healthy

Relationship

A PRACTICAL APPROACH

STEVE McCORD, MFT **& ANGIE McCORD,** CC

CENTRAL RECOVERY PRESS

CENTRAL RECOVERY PRESS

Central Recovery Press (CRP) is committed to publishing exceptional materials addressing addiction treatment, recovery, and behavioral health care topics, including original and quality books, audio/visual communications, and web-based new media. Through a diverse selection of titles, we seek to contribute a broad range of unique resources for professionals, recovering individuals and their families, and the general public.

For more information, visit www.centralrecoverypress.com.

Central Recovery Press, Las Vegas, NV
© 2011 by Steve and Angie McCord

ISBN-13: 978-1-936290-65-9 (paper)
ISBN-10: 1-936290-65-0

17 16 15 14 13 12 11   1 2 3 4 5

Publisher: Central Recovery Press
            3321 N. Buffalo Drive
            Las Vegas, NV 89129

EDITOR'S NOTE: The experiences and opinions expressed in this book are those of the authors only. To protect their anonymity, some of the names of people and institutions have been changed.

Cover design and interior layout by Sara Streifel, Think Creative Design

Dedicated to everyone who longs for love,
to anyone who seeks recovery from any addiction,
and in loving memory of Matthew Becnel,
who wasn't one of the lucky ones.

ACKNOWLEDGMENTS

This book would not have been possible without the many blessings we have received. We owe our lives, beyond our parents, to our spiritual ancestors Bill Wilson and Dr. Bob Smith, whose pain and vision were transformed into Alcoholics Anonymous, the foundation of all twelve-step programs. We are deeply grateful to those who came before us in our fellowships, our couples' community, and especially to those couples who generously contributed their stories.

We greatly appreciate the support we have received from our friends and family, and a special thanks to Antoinette for being the incentive for Angie to begin her recovery.

We acknowledge Central Recovery Press, its valuable mission, and our expert editor Valerie Killeen.

We are eternally grateful for the forces that brought us together and for the honor and privilege of trying to pass on what has been so freely given to us.

TABLE OF CONTENTS

PART II
Reality Bites: Living Together = Pouring Miracle-Gro on Character Defects

PART IV
Keeping the "I" in Marriage (When "for Me" = "for Us")

INTRODUCTION

Maybe you are one of those lucky men or women who arrived at adulthood emotionally and spiritually ready to step into and maintain a satisfying relationship with a life partner. Perhaps you grew up with two parents who were sufficiently healed from their own wounds, who could cope with the challenges of life, and who were physically and emotionally available for you. Maybe you feel that they had the intuitive ability to deliver what you needed throughout your upbringing. So, you searched for your life's partner with confidence and a sense of joy and anticipation, and now you are living happily ever after.

However, if this has not been your experience, this book was written for you, especially if you

- Have ever felt you were absent on the day they issued the instruction manual for how to have a relationship that is satisfying and successful (according to your personal definition).

- Have hungered for a life partner but don't know where to begin.

- Have had the courage and faith to risk stepping into one or more relationships that didn't turn out the way you had hoped.

- Are currently in a relationship that could be enhanced or taken to the next level, though you don't know how.

We ourselves had each concluded that perhaps we could not have a healthy partnership with a member of the opposite sex. We had both experienced pain, failure, loneliness, and yearning around our desire for a committed love relationship. For many years, we each worked individually on a spiritual program of recovery from addiction. We each achieved full and useful lives as single people. We came together later in life (at ages fifty-four and forty-four) in a way that we see as divinely guided, first as friends with growing respect and admiration for one another. A strong attraction developed, and we eventually began exploring the intimidating possibility of having a committed relationship with each other.

We then entered a couples community and were inspired by the stories of amazing people (some of which are included in Part V of this book). In some of these marriages, one or both spouses had abused substances or engaged in other destructive behavior for many years prior to recovery. We saw marriages that survived despite addiction, infidelity, death of children, and other seemingly insurmountable obstacles. We thought, *here are our healthy role models; these people must really know something about forgiveness. If they could do it, we could do it.* We felt hope for achieving what we wanted from a relationship. We took our place in that community, first in our dating stage, and then as a married couple. After a period of time, we began to see how our experience could also benefit others.

We take great joy in sharing our story and offering hope to single people, especially those who are just beginning the recovery journey. Often substance abuse has destroyed relationships, and people enter into recovery with baggage based on their past diseased actions. We offer encouragement that one can move into a position to have a successful relationship by putting the spiritual program of recovery first, praying for God's will, trusting a higher power, practicing spiritual principles, and being of service.

We also love working with other couples and sharing how we have used tools and spiritual principles to achieve and maintain a happy and contented marriage. That is why we wrote this book—to share our experience in order to help others and to pass along what has been freely given to us.

PART I

What It Was Like:

From Desolation to

"Happily Ever After"

1

ANGIE'S STORY

{ *Looking for love in all the wrong places until my real "Prince Charming" arrived* }

I was born on February 17, 1947 in Pasadena, California—or so they tell me; I really don't remember. I have paperwork and no reason to believe in a conspiracy theory, so I take this to be a fact. I was raised in an alcoholic home. Although my father was an alcoholic, there was love in our home. He was prone to occasional rages and sometimes passed along the shame that was given to him by his critical parents. He never physically abused us and did have some admirable qualities, not the least of which was his sense of humor.

In grade school kids made fun of me starting in fifth grade, when a kid named Peter told other kids not to touch my books because I had "cooties." This type of treatment persisted through eighth grade, when Glenn said he didn't think I was so bad, but he couldn't afford to be seen talking to me too much because it was such a burn. Funny thing, but I took that as a compliment. Then in ninth grade my family moved, so I went to a new school. I was devastated. That was the beginning of a series of events that, at the time, seemed to be the worst things that could possibly happen, but turned out to be the best. At the new school, no one knew I was supposed to be a creep. Kids were nice to me, and I grew up to be homecoming queen. I felt like the ugly duckling that turned into a swan.

I married when I was seventeen. I always liked to say that I married an older man (he was eighteen). He had been captain of the football team, and we rode off into the sunset to have a perfect life.

We got married in Las Vegas on New Year's Eve in 1964. On August 13, 1965, our daughter was born. Mr. Wonderful had a hard time settling down, and around February of 1969, he left us to live in a fraternity house. I was twenty-two years old, and it was clear that I was not going to have a perfect life, since I was facing divorce.

That is when I began drinking addictively. I went out with several guys, and for a while I had a nice boyfriend to whom my daughter became attached. When we broke up, I became involved with an abusive young man. I was worried for my daughter's safety and was relieved when the time came for her annual visit to my former in-laws in Texas. My drinking escalated, and I left my job to run away from that boyfriend. When I finally got away from him, I actually missed him! I had become very sick. My condition continued to deteriorate. For a time, the only reason that I did not consider myself homeless was because I still had a car. I allowed my daughter to live with her father. Her stepmother took good care of her.

I, however, experienced the worst period of my life. Finally I got it together enough to go back to work. I went out with a series of men who did not treat me well. Then I had a good relationship for about six months, and after that I didn't date much. My daughter came back to live with me. I drove drunk with her in the car and was powerless to stop, despite the remorse and horror I experienced. I was also having an affair with a married man. (I do not condone this behavior; I share it despite my shame in case someone may identify and find hope for recovery and healthy relationships despite serious past mistakes.) I became addicted to amphetamines and was on a ten-year diet, where I actually hoped that I would not lose so much weight that I could no longer get pills from the diet doctor. I finally hit bottom and admitted I was an addict. I thought that was the worst thing that could have happened to me, especially because I never wanted to be like my father in that regard. But I was wrong. It was absolutely the best thing, and the beginning of a new and wonderful life.

I got into recovery on June 26, 1978. My healing was slow. Initially I had intermittent, frustrating relationships, and then I was alone for long periods of time, once for four-and-a-half years, and another time for more than six years. During that time, I grew in many ways. I would have preferred to have had a man in my life, but I was not willing to settle. I worked a program of recovery and was of service to others. I concentrated on raising my daughter and learning to be a good employee and daughter. I began traveling all over the world with recovery groups. I prayed for God's will continuously. I followed whims, such as taking up belly dancing, swing dancing, and country western dancing. I bought a condo. I was having a great life, alone.

I reached the point where I figured that you either believe there is someone for you or you don't— either way, the solution is the same. You may as well get out and enjoy your life, because this is it. You do not want to look back and think you wasted your time being miserable.

I was enjoying my life, but still had the yearning to be in a special relationship with a man. I prayed. I made lists of qualities I desired in a mate. I learned to

1. **Be alone.** It's okay! As long as you have your health, family and friends who care about you, and enough money to do some things that you enjoy, you can have a great life. Sometimes I think there is not enough support for a single lifestyle.

2. **Be self-supporting**. I've always found it sad when people stay in miserable relationships because they are financially dependent on the other person.

3. **Be celibate**. I concluded that I could go the rest of my life without sex, but I could not go the rest of my life without self-esteem. I could no longer be with anyone who did not care about me.

4. **Say no to what I do not want.** This is half of the secret to getting what you *do* want. You have to be available when it comes along.

5. **Put God first.** I prayed for God's will and for the power to carry it out. I learned to act in integrity with myself and my principles.

6. **Take a man at his word.** If he says he does not want to be in a relationship, thank him for the information and move on. (Many a woman has confided in me that she did not heed the "warning" given to her. She thought he didn't really mean it, or would change his mind when he found out how wonderful she was.) Also, if a man says he is faithful, believe him. It doesn't pay to be jealous, unless you have evidence not to trust him. And then, if you are wrong, it is his spiritual defect, not yours.

For many years it would have been my will to be in a long-term, healthy relationship, but God's will was different. I learned to feel good about myself, to have a full life, and to be happy being alone. I had a successful career. I mentored others, both professionally and in spiritual fellowships. I helped my mother when she became terminally ill. I gained self-esteem. I learned a lot about myself, and I had some painful relationship experiences that would later help me to have the healthy relationship for which I yearned.

Enter my real Prince Charming and the beginning of a new journey.

2

STEVE'S STORY

{ *From hurting to healing to helping* }

I t all started in kindergarten. There she was with her curly golden locks and enchanting smile, missing her front teeth—love at first sight. I longed for her attention. I schemed, the best a five-year-old can, but it was not to be. Thus the tone was set for the next many years.

Rough Patches on Icy Slopes

Adolescence was a challenging and awkward time for me. This is ideally when we develop personal values; communication skills; a deepening awareness about the world around us and within us; and effective ways to deal with stress, disappointments, and conflicts in relationships. What an order, even under the best of conditions! In making this transition from adolescence to adulthood, I was to be on the twenty-year plan.

I had no idea how to relate to peers, the opposite sex, and difficult authority figures. I also struggled to make my way through the mysterious high-school social structures, while meeting intensifying academic and athletic demands. Don't even get me started on the cruelties and complexities of the boys' locker room.

At the apex of the hormonal and emotional chaos going on within me, the chaos of substance abuse and my parents' divorce were unfolding around me, complete with domestic violence and financial hardship. As adolescence is a time of exploration and experimentation, I set out seeking a way to cope. Unfortunately, instead of striving toward constructive coping skills, I turned to alcohol and other drugs. In the beginning, I thought I had beaten the game. Now I was going to parties and having a good time, where before I had felt like a dork. It appeared as though I had found the magical elixir of life, a substitute for hard work and emotional risk. I had discovered a quick way to move from dis-ease and discomfort to ease and comfort.

I felt bulletproof. I loved feeling self-sufficient. I could dream bigger dreams and blow off disappointments. Little did I know I was falling deeper into the grip of a spiritual malady or soul sickness. More specifically, I was growing more and more disconnected from myself, my essential nature, my gifts, my heart, and the love within and around me. There was a sense of never feeling "at home," or comfortable in my own skin. I had developed a skittish mind that was working directly against my own spiritual well-being.

So looking back it makes perfect sense that from the starting point of a poor relationship with myself, my relationships with the opposite sex would have been laughable if they weren't so tragic. Dating always felt unnatural, strained, and scripted—like I was auditioning. So I went about my life with my radar up for "mutuality," that is, open to meeting and sharing time with someone with similar interests. Unfortunately, I grew less interesting as my preoccupation with partying increased.

As alcohol/drugs became my primary relationship, the isolation deepened. I pushed people away, becoming disconnected from others. I could, in fact, be in a room full of people and feel alone. Yet once that first drink slid down my throat and warmed my belly, I experienced the illusion of connection and being okay. I had lost a conscious contact with my creator. I felt my spirit and my will to live dying. On November 30, 1988, I received the gift of desperation, and on December 1, 1988, I set out on a journey of recovery. Having always been fascinated by what makes people tick and relationships work or fail, I eventually set out to become a licensed marriage and family therapist. I was drawn to the mystery of the dance between the masculine and the feminine, which has been going on for hundreds of generations. I have worked in various settings, including private practice, public agencies such as children's services and an emergency psychiatric unit, and now a major health care provider. I eagerly studied and began observing the issues that can cause strife in a relationship, from poor communication to major differences in life values, goals, and ability to be emotionally intimate.

Getting Ready for Angie

I would see her at gatherings. I remember thinking whenever she walked in, "Oh good, Angie's here." I looked forward to hearing her talk. Frequently she would say something brilliant or witty. I would feel her raw honesty stretch a magical tendril through a small gap in my armor and touch my heart. I'd be caught off guard with a resonating truth, and overcome with belly laughter. And this was at a time in my life where absolutely nothing was funny. Nothing had been funny for quite a while.

When I first started to acknowledge my attraction to Angie, a mean-spirited voice inside convinced me that she was out of my league. What would this smart, beautiful, funny, and successful woman want with a guy like me? Then the medicine of the language of the heart began to heal me.

Ironically, at that time I was studying the wisdom of indigenous cultures and the notion of right action based on right timing and right position. A huge issue for me had always been trust; I didn't trust a soul. I didn't trust women. I didn't trust men. In fact, I didn't trust myself to know whom or what to trust. One of my mentors is fond of saying, "Don't start till you're ready, don't quit till you're done." Looking back, it was perfect that I did not have the confidence to approach Angie. I had some maturing to do—some vital, painful, wisdom-infusing, transformative life experiences—to help get me ready for Angie.

Another mentor taught me that a mature man needs to know two things:

1. Where am I going?

2. Who will go with me?

It is vital that I not get these two in the wrong order. If I make a substance or a woman my higher power, I am inviting massive misery into my life. I'm also asking any woman I get involved with to settle for a boy instead of a man. It is clear looking back that Spirit was still getting us ready for each other. It took some time to create the optimal circumstances that ultimately brought us together.

When the Student is Ready. . .

I suffered the excruciating results of trying to manage my own life armed only with a misguided self-will, half-hearted goals, a distorted perception of the world, and the emotional neediness of a two-year-old. Then I was drawn to a spiritual teacher. John had a peace about him, an infectious laugh, and a sparkle in his eye that intrigued me. How was it that his light burned so bright? How did this come about? He began to share with me what was shared with him. He taught me spiritual principles and how to practice them in everyday life. Together we began a journey that quickly yielded favorable results. The first miracle occurred in my work life. My trust in John and his teachings deepened. I began to feel a love and gratitude for him that scared me.

One day I realized that I'd take a bullet for John, which surprised me because I don't even like bullets.

Accepting Being Alone

"I just want someone to hold me while I isolate." –Anonymous

I remember driving with John to Santa Cruz one Thanksgiving to visit friends and saying how I felt hopelessly single. After a series of painful experiences, it appeared to me that I was incapable of being in a healthy relationship. John replied that, yes, there were some of us who may never have that. I felt myself surrender to this possibility. I began to find it acceptable, if that were going to be the reality for my life. He left me to reflect on the following: "It's not about finding the right person, it's about being the right person."

How We Got Together

On Sunday mornings after a weekly event, about a dozen of us would go out for coffee and chat. I would see Angie across the circle, wave, and say hello. Next thing I knew we began sitting next to each other, talking every week about our lives. Eventually, we were usually the last to leave. I was impressed with how Angie responded to her challenges in the workplace or with loved ones. Here was a bright, loving woman with impeccable integrity. My respect and trust deepened. I valued her take on things. She appeared interested in my point of view. We became friends. She was amused that I had once been engaged to be married—for three days. I grew curious about a long-distance relationship she had had with a man in Hawaii.

Then I felt an attraction developing. Our good-bye hugs kept getting longer and longer. When I would run into her twenty minutes later in Trader Joe's, I would think to myself, "Does this mean I can get another good-bye hug?" Once we got together to play a board game, and one night, purely to satisfy my curiosity about a new TV show, I went to Angie's because, after all, she had cable. Eventually I tested the waters by pondering out loud, "I wonder what would happen if we allowed ourselves to act on this attraction."

Here was a golden opportunity to blow the whole deal, to squash the newly formed tender shoot. We stood at a turning point. . .

Settling Before Settling Down

In the past I had settled—fallen into the arms of a woman who expressed interest, and my heart never had time to open before my zipper. And yet sex as a pathway to intimacy had repeatedly proven itself to be a dead end. A brief "courtship," turning up the heat before the relationship container grew strong enough to hold it, and then the passionate sex would blow it to pieces. One more time that awful feeling after the thrill is gone. Who is this stranger lying next to me, and are we truly compatible, beyond sexually?

Thankfully Angie shone the light of sanity and the evening ended simply with a long hug. I was clear that I did not want to do anything to jeopardize our friendship. I experienced a lot of ambivalence around taking the risk of becoming more than friends with Angie. Without realizing it, based on mutual respect and trust, Angie and I had been building the container of our relationship over years, unaware that someday it would be strong enough to hold the gathering strength of our erotic energy. With my relationship history, it was vitally important to me to open the door slowly, with full consciousness and clear intention versus lust-charged urgency. After living in the pain of unfulfilled hopes for a healthy relationship, we both appreciated that the magnificent opportunity for a life partnership does not come along every day.

Yikes, Now What?

On February 14, 2002, Angie and I attended our first couples retreat. Why? Because we were a couple. A couple of lunatics that is, as Angie's daughter once blurted out. She said, "You and Steve are both psycho, and it's a good thing that you are together, because you saved two other people from misery." Given our history of dismal relationships, we agreed that we needed all the help we could get. What a blessing the couples community has turned out to be.

The first year we attended, we were dating. The second year we attended, we were engaged. The third year, we were married. The sixth year, we led the damn thing! How could this be? How does this happen?

3

REFLECTIONS FOR THE "TERMINALLY SINGLE"

{ *Affirmations for identifying desired qualities in a mate* }

By Angie

As I have indicated, I was single for many years, without dating. It used to infuriate me when people would say, "When you quit looking, that is when it will happen." I felt like saying something sarcastic like, "Really? Well for how many years at a time do I have to quit?" I'm sure I had quit looking for several years at a time. Once someone said, "I quit looking, and nine months later I got together with Jim." Great! Only nine months.

Sprinkled throughout my writing are benefits I got from being alone and how eventually the experience helped me to be in a healthy relationship. What I want to share here is my last "wish list" for a mate:

Dated 1/20/01

Someday, God, I would like a man who

• Has a sense of humor

• Likes to play

• Wants to be in a relationship with me and commit to it

• Is mutually attracted

• Wants to have a nice home

• Wants to travel and/or share a variety of fun things with me

• Has enough money to do so

• Has good values, is faithful

• Is crazy about me

• Is a good companion, likes to have discussions and listen too

• Is spiritual in his own way

• Is willing to work on the relationship

No heavy drinkers, please

Dancing optional

I found a copy of this list sometime after Steve and I got together. He certainly meets every one of my desired criteria. I also notice there is no mention of physical attributes. This is an area where I think people sometimes get hung up. I learned my lesson. I used to think my ex-husband was super attractive. After we had been married a while, I asked my best friend, "I used to think my husband was the cutest guy I'd ever seen, and now he looks ugly to me; has he changed or do I just hate him?" She said, "I hate to tell you this, but you must hate him because he looks the same to me." I actually had to pray to be open and to give good-looking men a chance because I was so afraid they would be unfaithful. In fact, when Steve and I first started dating, I said, "God, I didn't need one this cute, but I'll take him!"

I was going through a painful relationship breakup about a year and a half before Steve and I started dating. I remember that someone gave me a list of affirmations regarding attracting a perfect companion. I loved using affirmations because they made me feel peaceful and hopeful. Therefore, I am including some affirmations on the following page to help single people who long for true love. Before Steve and I got together, I especially liked an affirmation about being in a partnership where we would love each other's ideas. This definitely applies to our relationship, because we started out as friends and the attraction grew slowly. Later, I will talk about "what I like about you" lists that Steve and I gave to each other when we were first dating. When I look back at those lists, I see that there are some substantive attraction factors (having to do mostly with internal qualities, character traits, and values we admired). And, as I recall the experience, we truly did love each other's ideas.

Affirmations

I deeply and completely love
and accept myself exactly the way I am.

I am lovable every moment of every day,
and I am worthy and ready for true love.

My ideal mate will be attracted to
my radiant inner beauty and ideas.

The universe is attracting to me a mate
with whom I am in perfect harmony.

I am co-creating with my higher power a true
and loving partnership that will serve others as well.

I joyfully attract a mate who is spiritual, prosperous, and fun.

My soul mate is preparing now to be in a relationship with me.

The true love of my life and I are irresistibly attracted
to each other physically, emotionally, spiritually,
and intellectually; we love each other's ideas.

We share core values, such as fidelity, honest
communication, trust, commitment, financial responsibility,
and dedication to a spiritual way of life.

We find great pleasure in each other's company; we make each
other laugh and treat each other with consideration and kindness.

We love and support each other unconditionally.

Our partnership magnifies the good in both of our lives and
in the lives of those to whom we would be of service.

I am cherished in the way I have always longed to be cherished,
and I cherish my partner in return.

I NOW ACCEPT THE SOUL MATE THAT
GOD IS GETTING READY FOR ME.

FROM SEEKING THE RIGHT PERSON
TO BECOMING THE RIGHT PERSON

{ *From self-centeredness to centered selfness* }

By Steve

It would be hard for me to find an area in my life that has resulted in more pain than physically intimate relationships. It's been said that getting into a relationship is like pouring Miracle-Gro on your defects of character. That described my experience.

The cycle consisted of growing sick of being alone; launching a hunt for "her"; doing whatever it took to succeed in the capture; indulging in the rapture of my new love object; ignoring, rationalizing, and dismissing all red flags; allowing my pain meter to rise to 9.99 out of 10; and then concocting my exit strategy. After shocking my bewildered mate with my disappearance, I would retreat to my cave to lick my wounds, feel sorry for myself, and bemoan the sad state of affairs—until loneliness became intolerable and I'd start the cycle all over again.

My pain intensified as I became more conscious of the pain I was causing others by my reckless pursuit of getting my needs (my wants, really) met. I was baffled and grew despondent as I observed others who seemed to pull off this mystical phenomenon of living in true partnership. Why was this seemingly impossible for me? What was I missing? What was I doing wrong?

I found it necessary, with some strong encouragement from a spiritual adviser, to take a long break and find out who Steve was without a partner. I recall nights of skin-crawling agony, hungering for companionship and simple human touch. It felt like going through a physical withdrawal, an emotional detoxification from a powerful drug.

It was deflating to face the reality that my entire relationship strategy had been exposed as not just ineffective, but harmful to me and others. I was challenged to take an in-depth personal inventory and examine my motives and the patterns that had played out in twenty-plus years of frustrating relationships. I had been coming from self-centeredness rather than centered selfness.

It was easy to rush to satisfy sexual hunger, and when I did, awareness arose that hunger remained—the hunger to love and be loved. It became undeniable that no matter how powerful or delicious the erotic energy between a man and woman, to build the foundation of a relationship on it is pure folly. For example, one Tuesday I was seated next to my sponsor waiting for a meeting to begin. Then *she* walked in—the woman I had been tumultuously dating off and on for the past year or so. My sponsor turned to me and said, "Your drug just walked into the room."

It was difficult to admit and then accept that our relationship had characteristics of addiction: soaring highs followed by crashing lows, life-disrupting preoccupation, the frenzied pursuit, being under the influence of adrenaline and endorphins, starry-eyed gazing into each other's eyes, an intoxicating sense of invincibility, then reality rudely imposing. It became clear that I could take the hook out of a substance or activity and put the hook into another person. I could get high from the dramatic ups and simulate the detoxing lows in a relationship, rather than seeking power from true source or higher power.

We seem to be biologically hardwired toward individuality and a drive to follow our own instincts—to feel, think, and act for ourselves, independently of others. And the plot thickens: we also seem to be biologically hardwired to yearn for closeness, to connect with another person, and to experience togetherness. A successful relationship allows for both of these needs of individuality and connectedness to be met. This requires a healthy sense of self and effective communication skills, as well as the ability to identify and express one's needs, set boundaries, negotiate compromise, and handle conflict. The good news is that these skills can be learned. For me that means being willing to have self-will aligned with God's will, praying for God to help shape my ideals around intimate relationships, and growing toward them.

I shifted my focus from *looking for* the right person to *being* the right person.

5

RELATIONSHIP WISH LIST

{ *Daring to dream: visioning qualities you want in a relationship* }

By Steve

I n gathering information for this book, I noted with interest an "ABC" list I'd written of what I dreamed of having in a relationship. It was dated 1994. I had a lot of learning, growing, and surrendering to do before this dream became a reality.

ABCs

Authenticity

Being who you are in the here and now

Consciousness, committed to realness

Compassion and creativity

Dynamic, change is embraced

Equality and ego surrender

Emotional baggage—observed, discussed, released

Expectations are discussed

Forgiveness flows

Gratitude grows

Honor gifts and differences with humility

Illusion of security, permanence is released

Love freely extended and received

Maintain individual identities, interests, friendships

No attacking, blaming

Open communication and ownership of issues

Outdoors time is important

Playfulness and passion is freely expressed

Purpose of individual and relationship aligned

Resentments aren't stored or scored

Spiritual and sexual compatibility

Transcend conditioning and compulsive commands of our lower self

Trust in ourselves, leading to trust in other

Use challenges to grow together vs. apart

Willing to be vulnerable

Zaniness has its place

EXERCISE

Take the time to write down what qualities are most important to you in a mate and in a relationship. Review your list periodically. "To thine own self be true."

6

DO YOU WANT A LIFE PARTNER?

{ *Daring to hope it is possible* }

By Steve

"D o you want a life partner?"

How's that for a question to be asked on a first date? I was stopped dead in my tracks when hit with this question by a woman I met at Esalen Institute in Big Sur, California. "Of course, I don't expect you to know whether that would be me or not; I just want to know if that's what you truly want for yourself," she said.

For some reason it never occurred to me to sidestep her question. I felt compelled to give her an honest answer. Hell, I wanted to know the answer to this question for myself after being a devout fence-sitter most of my life. The cons of commitment always seemed to outweigh the pros. I saw commitment as loss of freedom, rather than opportunity for greater freedom—the freedom to open my heart and love and be loved, the freedom from a wandering eye, musical lust, the constant hunt, and wondering, *might she be the one?*

It was safe to say that I had been strongly affected by the examples of marriage I saw from when I was a young boy up until that point in my life. I didn't see a single long-term, committed relationship that made me say, "Oh yes, I want that." I saw nasty arguments over petty stuff, verbal attacks, manipulation, vindictiveness, parents enduring misery to stay together "for the kids," passions abandoned to placate one's never-grateful spouse, betrayal, infidelity, black eyes, bouts of sobbing, and coffee mugs hurled across the kitchen—all this by the age of sixteen.

In my twenties there were times that I longed for, dreamed about, sought half-heartedly, and came close to being in a relationship. I would waffle, weasel, hem, haw, and always retreat. Yet, standing with this compelling northern Californian woman under a giant pine tree and watching the sun sink into the Pacific Ocean, I was given the gift of fresh eyes to look at this proposal. Now having had several years of squeezing every last drop of advantage from being single, I had to admit I was thirsty to taste what lifelong lovers enjoyed.

Was I willing to take the risk of admitting I wanted something that very well could be beyond my reach? My hope that a satisfying partnership could be possible seemed to be a hair stronger than the pessimism that it was impossible. My answer was yes; I wanted a life partner.

Now I was sitting in acceptance that I wanted a life partner, alongside the awareness that I didn't have one. Before long it was clear that Tanya and I were not to be life partners, but then I started thinking about a woman right in my own backyard—Angie.

REFLECTION

Can I take the risk today of allowing myself to know what I want?

7

OVERCOMING FEAR

{ *Two wolves—*
which will you feed? }

By Steve

Two Wolves

Author unknown

There once lived a boy in a mountain village. The boy began visiting the village elder and one day noticed an ornately hand-carved wooden medallion hanging from the elder's neck.

The boy studied the medallion and said it looked like there were two wolves. "Very good," said the elder, "Yes there are two wolves." The elder went on to explain that one wolf represented the force of creation and all that supports life in the world (love-based thought and action)

*and the other wolf represented the force of destruction and
all that threatens life (fear-based thought and action).*

*The boy leaned closer and saw that the wolves seemed to be fighting.
"Right again," said the elder. "Yes there is a great fight going on between
the force of creation and the force of destruction. We can see this fight
in the world between nations, in communities, between cultures, in
families, and guess what? There is even a great fight between these two
forces within the heart of every man and the heart of every woman."*

*Now the boy's face took on a look of intense anticipation as
he asked, "Well which wolf is going to win?"*

*The elder replied, "The one that we feed. You see, every thought
we think, every word we speak, each decision we make, every
action we take, each situation or relationship we put or find ourselves
in has within it the potential to either feed the wolf of creation
or the wolf of destruction. Choose mindfully."*

For many years, even if I had been aware of this truth, most likely I
would not have wanted to accept the responsibility. But now having
been initiated into manhood, leaving excuses and victim-thinking
behind, it was liberating and empowering to stand in this new place
of self-responsibility.

Now, with the spiritual principles I had been taught; the support
of mentors, a community of men, and trustworthy friends; and a
conscious contact with a power greater than myself that was growing
more solid as I showed up for life each new day, I no longer felt like I
was going to a gunfight with a pea-shooter.

Fear began to take a backseat, rather than being a driving force in my
life. I no longer felt intimidated in the company of a powerful woman.
The mean-spirited inner voice had been quieted. I had more courage
to take healthy risks.

"Maybe I will ask Angie out on a date," I thought.

8

INFATUATION OR INTIMACY

{ *A bird may love a fish,*
but where would they live? }

Reflections on areas of compatibility
By Steve

Infatuation = false fire

Intimacy = into the fire/willingness to let heat build. Two people taking the risk of revealing the truth about themselves with each other… "Into me you see."

Sex and relationships are often confused as being one and the same. Yet sex can be as primal as two bodies rubbing against each other until enough pleasure has been had, then moving on and never looking back. Sex doesn't necessarily involve intimacy. In fact, sex can be used to avoid intimacy. Intimacy doesn't necessarily involve sex. I've experienced incredible intimacy that involved zero erotic energy or physical contact. So often in the media we see sex portrayed as the path to an intimate relationship. The foundation, the starting point is depicted as torrid, uncontrollable lust—never mind whether compatibility extends beyond pheromones. Damn the torpedoes, full speed ahead, we'll figure out later whether we truly have the makings of an adult relationship.

It was essential that I learned to say no to the temptation of any relationship based on physical attraction alone, which is an immature selection criterion. If I choose to participate in a relationship that is not based on adult-to-adult relating, I am swimming in a muck of dominance and dependence, either playing the parent or the child role at any given moment. I have seen gross manipulation conducted under the banner of love. Sometimes the most loving action we can take toward another or ourselves is to say no and not cave in.

EXERCISE

The questions below may be helpful in evaluating whether you really want to get involved with someone…before the clothes come off.

REFLECTION/AREAS OF COMPATIBILITY

• Do I like this person?

• Do I respect/admire this person?

• Is there attraction/chemistry?

• Do I have a sense of ease and comfort with this person?

• Am I able to communicate my feelings?

• Are we intellectually compatible?

• Do we have overlapping interests?

• Are our spiritual values compatible?

• Do we share common goals?

• Can we add to each other's lives?

Every spiritual path begins with acknowledging what is true in this moment. If I can't find the truth right here, right now, where do I expect to find it?

9

MY MAGIC MAGNIFYING MIND

{ *What I like about you* }

By Angie

Over the many years I was single and not in a relationship, I had occasion to mentor women and to try to help friends who sought my counsel. When a friend complained frequently to me about her partner, it occurred to me that at some point there must have been something she liked about him, or they would not have been together. My advice to her: write a list of what you like about him, his good qualities. Focus on that list. Read it again for several days in a row and keep adding anything else positive you might think of. Now I think that advice must have been channeled through me, as I had very little positive relationship experience on which to base it!

Steve and I met in a spiritual recovery program. We became friends and confidants. We used to go to coffee on Sundays with a group, and pretty soon our conversations got longer and longer, and our hugs got longer and longer (Steve tells this better). This went on over a period of about two years. In June of 2000, I meditated about him, wondering if I should make the first move. I got that he was not that shy, and I sensed that it was not appropriate for me to initiate in this instance; therefore, if he did not come forward, it was not going to happen. (In retrospect this was a wise decision, which you can see in Steve's story; his apparent ambivalence was not about shyness, but his deliberate work toward wanting to approach relationships in a healthier way.)

For someone who takes charge and likes her ducks in a row, this was difficult. I prayed for God's will. My friend saw us together and said, "He really likes you. I can see it when he looks at you." I said, "Yeah, I know all about it!" Obviously I felt that too, but was frustrated that he never took the first step. Around December of 2000, he called to tell me he was not available. He said that he felt that when he flirted he was communicating a message that he was available, but he was not. We agreed not to act on our mutual attraction. However, I felt that he was conflicted. But I had finally learned that I did not know what was good for me; I'd even listed in my journal the names of guys I had been attracted to whom I now thought were jerks.

I prayed and prayed, but I did not pray for Steve and me to be together. Instead, I continued to pray for God's will. Steve and I continued to see each other at our coffee gatherings and to do things together occasionally.

On July 4, 2001, he finally asked me for a real date. We went out on Saturday, July 6, 2001 to a concert. I remember thinking that if there were never anything else, that night was enough. At that time, if you had told me I could spend one night a month into the future with someone with whom I felt the way I felt about Steve, I would have been overjoyed.

After we had been dating about a month, we had a conversation in which we affirmed that we would be dating each other exclusively. Shortly thereafter, we had our first real kiss. This was a monumental moment in our history. Our relationship had built up so slowly, and we already had feelings for each other, along with the prior painful relationship experiences. We both wanted to do things differently. Speaking for myself, I had been afraid to kiss him.

Shortly after, on the morning of August 3, I felt compelled to write a list of what I liked about Steve. I got to work early and typed up the list before the work day started. I think I sensed that this was going to be a very important relationship, and I wanted to remember the good things, just as I had been advising my friends to do. Steve and I spoke that night. I cannot remember which of us brought it up first; however, when we talked that night, I found out that he had written his own list that same morning of what he liked about me. We were probably writing those lists at the same time, and we never discussed writing these lists before we had each written one and shared it with each other. Also, looking over them now, I am struck that they each have sixteen items. What synchronicity! (Does that sound like God's will?)

We carried this into our relationship, and about once a year we write new "what I like about you" lists. It has gotten harder over the years because it does not seem like there is anything new, but these lists reaffirm our ongoing love, and our expressions of appreciation are often at a deeper level. I once suggested this to a friend who said that her partner would never do anything like that. I suspect that even if one partner gave the other a "what I like about you" list, it would be beneficial for the relationship. In my experience, it is more important for me to give love rather than worry about what I am or am not getting. And when a person receives love, he or she is more likely to feel like giving love rather than protecting him- or herself. The person may not return love in exactly the same way, but I cannot imagine that the effect would not be more positive than negative.

PRAYER

Dear God, today please help me to express love and appreciation freely, even when I am afraid it will not be returned.

EXERCISE

Make a list of what you like or love about your partner. Read it a few times a day, adding to it as inspired, for one week. At the end of the week, give the completed list to your partner. Do this even if your partner will not do the same.

10

CONFUSION OF NEEDS AND THE THREE CIRCLES OF SELF-AWARENESS

{ *Honestly facing and discussing "must haves" and "deal breakers"* }

By Steve

For so many years I was a misguided seeker. I went after things that I thought would fulfill me, only to remain discontented. I also would avoid things that I later discovered were actually in my best interest to include in my life.

What happens when two people who don't know what they want get together? They are likely to breed confusion or worse—perpetually unmet expectations, frustration, disappointment, and resentment.

When I began discussing my interest in Angie with a mentor, he suggested that I become armed with some vital information about myself. Who is this guy Steve I may be about to bring to a relationship? My mentor taught me that who I am is in part defined by my wants and needs, my "yeses" and "nos."

I was to take a piece of paper and draw three concentric circles:

- In the innermost circle, I was to list that which I "must have" in my relationship—the positive "deal breakers."

- In the middle circle, I was to list "strong desirables."

- In the outer circle, I was to write my "preferences."

On the back side of the paper, I was to draw three more concentric circles:

- In the innermost circle, I was to list "up with which I will not put"—the negative "deal breakers."

- In the middle circle, I was to list "strong dislikes."

- In the outer circle, I was to write my "annoyances."

The "must have" and "up with which I will not put" items were non-negotiable.

This exercise forced me to examine my personal truths. It put me in position to be able to offer my potential life partner someone who knows who he is. And because part of what I wanted was to be with someone who knows who she is as well, I invited Angie to do the exercise. We then compared notes and discovered a high degree of compatibility.

Angie adds:

I was terrified when Steve asked me to do this exercise. Now, I am grateful. I have known friends who got married without having discussed things as critical as their spiritual values or how they were going to handle their money. I appreciated Steve's desire to approach our relationship consciously.

I thought it might be helpful to share our actual lists as an example. These make great discussion points. And, I was so relieved to discover that many of the things that were important to me were also important to Steve. (We have shown this exercise as columns, rather than as circles, for ease of comparison.)

ANGIE	STEVE
MUST HAVES	
• Spiritual base • Shared values (fidelity, honesty, trust, consideration, and kindness) • Enjoy each other's company and doing things together (share interests) • Sense of humor • Mutual attraction (desire/ sex life) • Financial independence • Wants to be in a relationship with me, and willing to work at it • Basic compatibility	• We're willing to grow along spiritual lines • Common purpose for relationship–supportive of each other's spiritual progress • Our relationship glorifies God • We reveal our true selves in conscious partnership and accept "whole package" of the other • We practice honest communication, stay current, conflicts discussed • We treasure, protect, and deepen our mutual trust • We enjoy each other, including simple harmonious companionship • We add to each other's lives • We have some shared interests and goals

continued on page 39

ANGIE	STEVE
STRONG DESIRABLES	
• Program (of recovery)	• We laugh together and don't take ourselves too seriously
	• We enjoy physical closeness, apartness, and side-by-sideness
	• We're both willing to lead, follow, and/or walk side-by-side through the fire of two powerful hearts opening to each other
	• We co-create together, to add to the world around us and just for the fun of it
	• We both support partnership (i.e., financial security)
PREFERENCES	
• Dancing would be nice	• We dance together, cook together
	• If one of us needs some solitude, we can just ask
UP WITH WHICH I WILL NOT PUT	
• Drunkenness	• Violence or threats of violence
• Compulsive gambling (financial recklessness)	• Infidelity
	• Relationship that worsens my partner's or my spiritual condition, threatens recovery or sanity
	• Repeated emotional or financial recklessness

continued on page 40

ANGIE	STEVE
STRONG DISLIKES	
• Neglect and devaluing of the relationship • Anything in opposition to the "must haves"	• Important decisions (that affect relationship) made unilaterally • Demands vs. requests • Unspoken agreements, expectations that unexpressed needs be met • Angst for sake of angst, blaming vs. ownership of feelings • Too much attention on material, consumerism
ANNOYANCES	
• Reserving my time and then canceling, if it happens very often (when I could have done, or might have wanted to do, something else)	• Meddling family or friends • Cluttered living space • A lot of TV noise

PRAYER

Dear God, please give me the courage to face and discuss compatibility issues before jumping into a long-term commitment. Give me the faith and trust that if this relationship is Your will, it can survive honesty and discussion. May we do Thy will always.

11

THERE ARE NO RULES

{ *Baby steps from self-reliance to partnership* }

By Angie

When Steve and I started dating in 2001, I had been single since about 1969. I had not lived with a man since that time, and I could not envision how that would ever be possible for me. I came home from work dead-tired during the week, and could not imagine having to talk to anyone. I did whatever I wanted, spent my money however I pleased, went on trips with recovery groups, and had a successful career. In summary, I was quite independent. I had the desire in my heart to be in a life partnership, but could not picture the jump from where I was to living with anyone in that kind of romantic arrangement. Furthermore, how could I ever merge my finances with anyone else's?

Steve and I went to our first couples retreat in February of 2002, after we had been dating for about seven months. The retreat stimulated a discussion about intimacy and finances. I got the courage to tell Steve that I did not think I could ever be married because I could not co-mingle my finances with anyone after being independent for so long. I could not see myself going to someone and asking, "Honey, can I have a belly dance costume this year?" Steve said, "There are no rules. We're adults. We can make our own rules. I don't see why we couldn't have separate finances and then a pool for mutual expenses." His wisdom caused a huge shift. That felt doable to me. I began to see how maybe it would be possible for me to share my life with someone, and for us to work things out together.

PRAYER

Dear God, please help me to stay in the now and keep an open mind. No matter what I am going through, help me to remember that You are in charge. You are the creator and possessor of infinite wisdom that I cannot imagine until it is time for me to know. All I need to do is keep first things first, take the next step, do the right thing, and trust the process.

SPIRITUAL, PROSPEROUS,
AND FUN

{ *Kids with credit cards* }

By Steve

"**I** want a relationship that is spiritual, prosperous, and fun!"

When these words came out of Angie's mouth, I remember thinking, "Here is a wise woman with her head screwed on straight who speaks my language. This really sums up exactly what I want. Simply." We examined them and concluded that our spiritual values were compatible.

We both have demonstrated throughout our lives that we are financially responsible, capable of hard work, and effective at money management—yet we can let our hair down, not have to pinch pennies, be frivolous, and enjoy ourselves.

Our first New Year's together, we were in Big Sur, getting ready to drive home. We had intentionally left this last night of our long weekend open. We were driving south on Pacific Coast Highway. "What do you want to do? Where would you like to stay?" I asked. Angie said, "We could do anything we want; we're kids with credit cards!" We laughed hard, and I felt such a truth in those words. We ended up in a Jacuzzi in Santa Barbara, then played Scrabble after a fine meal.

GRATITUDE PRAYER

Dear God, thank you for putting someone in my life to share the same path. Thank you for giving us the ability to take care of business first so that we are free to enjoy our many blessings.

MISSION STATEMENT OF OUR COUPLESHIP

We passionately co-create a harmonious union that radiates joy and inspires community.

EXERCISE

Think about your relationship and discuss with your partner: if we were to have a mission, what would it be?

13

THE WHOLE PACKAGE

{ *Acceptance and commitment* }

By Steve

On a January morning, watching the snow fall and dust the two thousand-foot cliff faces in Yosemite Valley, I could already feel the medicine of Mother Nature working her magic. I put down my cup of Italian Roast coffee and resumed writing. It was as if I were excavating, removing all the rock to get to the gold, to the truth.

"I want no man before his time." Months prior, when I heard Angie speak these words, I felt my heart sing. I am attracted to this beautiful, sexy, successful, funny woman, who is also very wise. So many times

I felt the beginning of the end of a relationship before it even had a chance because of an undertow of urgency. Now I felt the freedom to breathe and allow the process to unfold. Angie and I were clearly moving toward taking our relationship to the next level. Again. From friendship and longing to dating to…marriage? Was it time to, not pop the cork, but the question?

I had chosen to leave the concrete and distractions of the city and listen to the Merced River and the winds rattle the bare branches of the aspen trees. If I want answers that are useful, if I want to maximize my chance of making a correct decision, it's helpful to know the right questions to ask.

So far I was batting zero. I was zero for one in the marriage proposal arena. In 1987, I made a decision to get married based on incomplete information about myself and my first wife. It wasn't long before I had to sit in the pain of not being able to live up to a serious commitment.

In order to step confidently into a sacred union with Angie, the questions I pondered were

1. Can I accept the whole package of this woman?

2. Do I trust that this woman accepts the whole package of me?

3. Do I know her?

4. Do I know myself?

What were my no-bullshit answers to be? I knew one thing: this awesome woman deserved to be with a man with both feet in. Was I truly willing to be all in?

Angie loves to tell the story of how I gave her a questionnaire when we started dating. This is described in the "Confusion of Needs and the Three Circles of Self-Awareness" story. I believe the time we both took to complete and share that self-inventory with each other was time well spent that now was about to pay dividends. Between that inventory, along with the areas of compatibility and all of our experiences so far, I could say yes to all four questions.

It was time to begin the drive home and shift to a whole new set of questions, like where and when shall we have the wedding?

14

MORE ABOUT GOD'S WILL

{ *Turning our will and lives over, together* }

By Angie

When I first got into recovery, I was so sick that I thought I was well. I thought I was already doing all of the steps and practicing all of the spiritual principles. There was one exception: it had never occurred to me that there was such a thing as God's will. I had been busy praying for *my* will—to make people do what I wanted. After a period of time I came to realize how little I actually knew. The longer I was in recovery, the less I knew. After several years, I occasionally thought I knew what God's will should be, and I was

handicapped by that "knowledge."

I had a stressful job with some negative circumstances. I was absolutely certain that it was not God's will for me to work there. God would not want me to live in negativity; I should know, after all, I had been in recovery and working a program for twenty-three years at the time. This was in October of 2002, when I began looking fervently for another position within the same system. Steve and I had been dating since July of 2001. I knew it was a serious relationship. In August of 2002, while on retreat, he had told me that he pretty much knew that he wanted to spend the rest of his life with me, but he thought he should wait until we had been officially dating for two years to propose.

I looked for a new job or transfer through the holidays and was becoming more and more anxious about not finding something. I was near retirement, but there were significant spousal benefits that applied if one was married for one year prior to retirement; therefore, I did not want to retire then get married afterward. However, I did not feel it was ethical in my line of work to take a job without the intent of making a two-year commitment. Time was running short; the system operated around March as the most desirable retirement month. Finally, early in January Steve asked what was bothering me. With much consternation, I told him what I was feeling, cried, and said I would work much longer if need be. A few days later, he came over and told me he thought we should get me retired. So, we decided in January of 2003 to get married in March of that year. He moved into our home in February. Two or three weeks after we had decided to get married, his landlord came by and told him he would have to move. We were amazed. Had we not already decided to get married and move in together, this might have been a problem, as Steve would have been without a place to live, and we might have felt pressed to make some decisions about our future. It seemed like perfect timing.

It was such a happy ending. My will had been to find a new job. Instead, I stayed with the old job until I retired in March, one year after we married. Had I gotten the new job, I would not have had that discussion with Steve, and we would have gotten married much later. We were grateful not to have had a long engagement. We both had a great deal of fear about living together and ruining a terrific relationship. We were spared the prolonged agony and fear of anticipating that event. We both felt that we did not need to live together prior to getting married, and that, with God's help, it would work if we both wanted it. And we both wanted it.

The first time we needed to discuss something that was scary and emotionally-charged for both of us, Steve suggested that we first say the prayer to turn our will and lives over to God, substituting the words "I" and "me" with "we" and "us." It was amazing how the energy changed. It felt as if, instantly, peace flowed into and guided our discussion. We still pray before sensitive discussions.

PRAYER*

God, we offer ourselves to Thee, to build with us and to do with us as Thou wilt. Relieve us of the bondage of self, that we may better do Thy will. Take away our difficulties, that victory over them may bear witness to those we would help of Thy power, Thy love, and Thy way of life. May we do Thy will always!

AND THEY LIVED HAPPILY EVER AFTER

(Hey—not so fast! Please read on.)

---

*Adapted from the Third Step Prayer in *Alcoholics Anonymous*.

PART II

Reality Bites:

Living Together =

Pouring Miracle-Gro

on Character Defects

RESTLESS, IRRITABLE, AND DISCONTENT

{ *Recognizing and owning our own moods and negative tendencies* }

By Angie

W ithout a doubt, being alone for several years taught me valuable lessons that enable me to be in a healthy relationship today. Once in a while, I catch myself feeling disgruntled and thinking critically about Steve, thoughts that begin with "he" and end negatively about something he does or, worse yet, what I imagine he might say or do (which is unfair, to say the least). Fortunately I am able to recognize that it is about things that don't normally bother me. Besides, it is a familiar feeling and one that reminds me of a funny but useful experience.

In the early nineties I was engaged to a man who lived in Hawaii; I lived in California. I had not talked to him for a couple of days. One morning I woke up and thought, "Damn him! If he had been here, he would have left his clothes all over the bedroom floor and expected me to pick them up. That jerk! And to think I even thought of marrying him."

Then I went off to work in a huff. The next day I was driving to work and thought, "Oh that Bob, he really is so sweet." Then it occurred to me that he had said or done nothing—nothing to make me angry and nothing to make me stop feeling that way. Had he been with me when I was in that mood, he could not have said anything right. And if he had not said anything at all, I would have been even angrier because he was "blowing me off."

REFLECTION

It is sometimes difficult to know when I need to keep quiet or discuss my feelings about something. It is useful to check within before speaking up: Is it just me? Should I wait to bring this up? When I wait, there is almost always another opportunity to talk, but when I say something I regret, I can't take it back.

PRAYER

Dear God, please guide me in knowing when to bring my concerns into the container of my relationship with my partner. Help me to know when it is better to first discuss the issue with a trusted friend. Please help me to be kind and loving to my partner at all times. Help me to treat him or her the way I would want to be treated.

HOW GOOD CAN YOU STAND IT?

{ *Navigating away from the trap of self-sabotage* }

By Steve

I'm sure most of us are familiar with a case where someone's life is going along rather smoothly, when out of the blue he or she does or says something that causes a big upheaval, conflict, or even a catastrophe. The term "self-sabotage" is sometimes used.

It is as if the person reached a point where he or she could no longer stand it "that good," and, rather than wait for the other shoe to drop, removed the suspense by pulling the rug out from underneath. It's almost like a thermostat where once the temperature gets to a certain level, the heat turns on automatically.

For whatever reason, I found myself teetering on the edge of such an opportunity a couple of years into our marriage. Never before in my life had I experienced such a long string of great weeks, unstrained months, and entirely acceptable years. It was bound to end, wasn't it? I've had a sense of impending doom before in my life. Looking back, I believe it was because doom was impending. This case was a totally different ball game. I grew restless at work. I started to negatively judge my home environment. I was eating foods that I know don't work well for me. I rebelled against my self-care instinct to exercise. I played with the idea of moving to the mountains. I observed all of this with curiosity, then alarm, as my half-hearted attempts to make changes fell short.

I caught myself fantasizing about being single again, purposefully focusing only on the benefits and conveniently overlooking the blessings of marriage. I started to privately question how Angie could be satisfied with me with all my quirks. I turned my magic magnifying mind onto her shortcomings. I felt a lull in my attraction to her and avoided lovemaking.

Well, I had never been here before. I had never been in a relationship long enough for this to happen. What was really going on? It's the ever-changing face of intimacy—the ebb and flow of closeness, attraction, desire, being emotionally available, and feeling that both feet are firmly rooted on the earth, much less in the relationship.

If a central purpose of relationship is to provide friction for spiritual growth, I was poised for one helluva growth spurt. A useful mantra at a time like this is "don't leave five minutes before the miracle…or five minutes after the miracle!" I didn't, and am glad to have passed on a perfectly good self-sabotage opportunity. (There will be more about this in Section Ten, "The Four R's of Relationship.")

3

HUMILITY

{ *For better or for worse,*
but not for lunch? }

By Angie

I don't know about you, but I was absolutely programmed to experience rejection. Even though I am much better now, in the past I had a tendency to take things personally or to feel rejected even when in reality that was not what was happening. When I first retired in 2004, I thought Steve would be deliriously happy for me, and that I would be in a Betty Crocker apron trying out new recipes. Don't get me wrong, he was enormously supportive—but there was also a surprise. His work schedule gave him a full day off during the week, and he worked only afternoon hours on a couple of other days. One day he told me that he needed a few hours a week alone in our home. What I heard was that I was not welcome in my own home. Then I had the thought, "You prayed to love him the way he needed to be loved, well here is your chance; all he is asking for is a little space."

I understand it now and do have my own space needs, but at the time it felt like rejection. I have had to work and pray for my character defects to be removed. One of the most painful of those defects has been taking things personally. I get comfort from a reading that was found on the desk of Dr. Bob Smith, one of the co-founders of Alcoholics Anonymous:

Humility

Perpetual quietness of heart. It is to have no trouble. It is never to be fretted or vexed, irritable or sore; to wonder at nothing that is done to me, to feel nothing done against me. It is to be at rest when nobody praises me. When I am blamed or despised, it is to have a blessed home in myself where I can go in and shut the door and pray to my Father in secret and be at peace, as in a deep sea of calmness, when all around and about is seeming trouble.

I consider this to be a good reminder and worthy aspiration, although at times impossible. Nonetheless, reading it does give me peace. I need to remember that we strive for progress, not perfection. Before recovery, it seemed like I was either the queen or the worm. I was either on top of the world or begging for a place to live in it. I joke that in school I got A's and D's. If I could not do something well, I didn't even want to try. What a joy and relief it has been to be content to be a worker among workers and to be right-sized (most of the time).

PRAYER

Dear God, please save me from needlessly getting my feelings hurt. Rather than taking things personally, please direct my attention to what You would have me do. Please let me focus on what I can add to any situation and help me to be of service to others.

4

THAR SHE BLOWS

{ *Surviving conflict* }

By Steve

O h no, here it comes!

Have you ever had that sinking feeling when you had that first fight in a relationship? After things had being going so well! A little voice says, "This is the beginning of the end."

When there was disagreement in my family, it was possible someone was going to get hurt or leave or both, or someone was going to be made to feel wrong, selfish, or ungrateful for seeing things differently or wanting something different.

Our first fight came one night when in anger, Angie loudly threw some salad dressing bottles into the trash bin. It startled me. It scared me. I had never seen Angie act that way. I had been complaining that there was not enough room in the refrigerator for my stuff. I sadly surmised that if there wasn't room for my stuff, if my stuff wasn't welcome in our living space, then maybe I wasn't welcome and should go elsewhere. An ominous mountain was crafted from a dingy molehill.

We both disliked conflict and had sought to avoid it. I think we were married a year and a half before we had our first fight. We could postpone the inevitable only so long. Here it was, time to face our fears. Thankfully we didn't fall into the trap of clinging to a position of blaming the other. We each owned and shared our feelings. It was a relief to know we could survive conflict.

REFLECTION

I don't have to believe everything I think.

5

SPACE VS. TOGETHERNESS

{ *More about humility* }

By Angie

I did not like being the person in the relationship who could handle more togetherness, and it took a while for me to adjust. First, I am the woman, and as such I believed Steve should be chasing after me and begging for my time. Second, knowing I desired more togetherness than my partner somehow diminished me and made me feel that my needs or wants were wrong. Third, it made me feel clingy, when I know I am not. I was (and am) a strong, independent woman.

There is nothing "wrong" with the wants and needs of either me or my partner, who needs more solitude than I do, especially as a writer. He needed so much, in fact, that I think at one time he perceived me as not having space needs. The truth is that I do have them and they are easily met, mostly because his needs are greater than mine, which automatically creates space for me. I have come to appreciate our life and patterns together very much. I love spending quiet time in the mornings, and taking trips where we don't have to talk for a few hours. I find it peaceful and enjoyable.

I was not always content with Steve's space needs. Earlier, in the section regarding humility, I talked about my tendency to take things personally. I also think I had what could be considered fear of abandonment. Steve, on the other hand, had a fear of engulfment, which means that he had issues with feeling smothered or being afraid of losing his self or identity in another person. It is an interesting dynamic. When the person who fears engulfment needs space, the person who fears abandonment may be tempted to move even closer, which in turn creates an even greater need for the other person to move away.

When I was feeling abandoned or unloved, it was wise on my part to give Steve distance until he was ready to "come out of his cave," reminding myself that he always emerged on his own, ready for closeness again. Had I instead moved closer, he would probably have felt the need for even greater distance. In working with others, I have noticed this to be a common dynamic in relationships. Ironically, as the years have gone by, Steve has felt the need for less and less alone time. We have both become more secure and settled into our marriage.

My transformation from hurt feelings to more fully enjoying my alone time has been satisfying. I relish my independence within the relationship. This change resulted from self-examination, prayer, discussion, and coming to understand that when Steve needs alone time, it is not an indication of decreased love, but rather a form of self-care that helps him to be able to express even more love. I have been able to adjust my expectations and even to embrace his alone time as good for our relationship. We both greatly enjoy the ebb and flow of space vs. togetherness, and we take pleasure in doing things on our own and then coming back together.

One of the things I found helpful during my adjustment process was a self-examination form that I received during a workshop. The form posed an interesting question: what is my belief about what a man's role should be, and what a woman's role should be? It became clear that holding unconscious expectations that my partner should behave in a certain way, based on gender, could be troublesome. Surprise!

When two people marry, the man brings his package of beliefs and rules about what a man is supposed to do, based on his upbringing and the role models in his life. This also applies to my expectations of my husband as a man, and of myself as a woman. In this example, my belief might be something like "real women are always chased after by men." Therefore, if my partner has greater space needs than I do, I am somehow not a "real woman." It is easy to see how such an unconscious belief could be a problem.

EXERCISE

In your journal or notebook, make a list of what you think a man's role should be and what a woman's role should be. For example,

Real men should always _____.

Real women should always _____.

If your partner is willing, ask him or her to do the same, and share your lists. Some interesting unconscious expectations or self-imposed pressures may be revealed. Remember that this applies not only to what each of us thinks our partner should do, but also to our expectations of ourselves.

6

STILL FLAWED AFTER ALL THESE YEARS

{ *Driving each other crazy*
(Who, us? Character defects?) }

By Angie

One of the biggest sources of disillusionment in recovery is about character defects or shortcomings. Anyone who expects all of them to be fully removed may be disappointed, to say the least. We can keep praying and being willing, or trying to become "entirely willing." In some instances, remarkable, and even seemingly miraculous improvement results. One tiny example is that prior to recovery, I was always a grouch in the morning. Later, I was mentoring a woman who called me at 5:30 a.m. every day. Some days I was still asleep when she called. I didn't want her to feel bad, so I would jump up and answer the phone in a cheerful voice as if I had been up for a while. After a time, I noticed that I was no longer a morning grouch. When I commented to my daughter, she agreed. I asked her exactly when that happened, but neither of us could pinpoint the date. So sometimes change can occur just from "acting as if," without us even realizing it at the time. (Now I get accused of having "spring-loaded pajamas" because I am such a morning person.)

Steve and I are abashed to think that anyone would assume, just because we wrote this book, that we are setting ourselves up as any kind of authority. Heaven forbid that anyone would conclude that we pretended to be without fault. We are both very efficient people, and we admire and love each other deeply. We are definitely not, however, without fault. At one time when Steve made a mistake, I reassured him by saying that it was important for him to make just enough mistakes so that he would not be insufferable when other people make theirs. He has since told me the same thing when I've made a mistake, and we have had a good laugh about it. You see, efficient people have special character defects, such as judgment, self-righteousness, and impatience. Why can't everyone do things the way I would? This thinking renders us far from perfect.

One of our favorite people, Irish Annie, who is now deceased, said that if you don't think you have character defects, spend time with your teenagers—if you don't have kids, rent some. Steve and I might say, "Get in the car with your partner." For us, this is what we would call an identified growth area.

Baby, will you drive my car?

By Steve

Not. I hate the term "control freak." I prefer to see myself as having clarity of intention and being passionately goal-oriented. And—I won't allow anyone to drive my car. I've tried to let go in this particular area, but no luck yet. There are also times it is difficult for me to be a passenger in another person's car. It's worse with some drivers than with others. This has been a source of conflict and challenge in Angie's and my relationship.

One night we decided to go to a bistro for dinner and to see a friend perform with his band. This trek meant driving through downtown Los Angeles during rush hour. One thing we both know is that I am better equipped to do the long-haul driving on road trips, and Angie has the temperament to better handle bumper-to-bumper traffic. If only I could let go and be a passenger. But no…this particular night, the traffic was a nightmare. I barked an order for Angie to get in the carpool lane where the traffic was moving better. She obeyed, but then got angry.

Driving can serve as a metaphor for the journey of living: trying to get somewhere, coping with obstacles to forward progress, aggression, encroachment of boundaries, yielding, and coping with sudden changes. We can only be so prepared, then there is nothing left to do but let go, cease fighting, and accept the things we cannot change. We agreed on a stress-reduction plan for the future:

• The driver decides on the route.

• Leave plenty of time for traffic or other delays.

• Double-check the directions before leaving, and have a good old-fashioned map.

• Pray when we get in the car.

• Be sure we have CDs of spiritual or recovery speakers to increase serenity when traffic is heavy.

Angie adds:

I love how Steve described driving as a metaphor for the journey of living. It is definitely an opportunity to respect feelings and differences. It was amusing that driving emerged as the topic at the opening open-format meeting at our last couples retreat. The leader laughed because she was going to choose it as an official discussion topic, but her partner did not think anyone would want to talk about it. We heard so many stories from other couples; it seems some people change once they get behind a wheel. Some referred to this as a "testosterone thing." I hate to gender-generalize, but it did seem that there were common experiences—usually the woman was the gasper and thought the man drove too fast or got angry or impatient behind the wheel.

Many couples admitted they fought over driving. So, we are not alone. And though our driving conflicts are far from resolved, there has been growth. For example, Steve used to think that when I acted startled that I just needed to trust him because he had full control of the car. Eventually, he realized that my gasps were an involuntary reaction and not a reflection on him.

Steve thought I drove too slowly and did not pay enough attention to what I was doing. Steve's approach was very goal-oriented. Once he got behind the wheel, he was on a mission to get there as efficiently as possible, even if there was plenty of time. He preferred to avoid obstacles to forward progress and to have open road in front of him; he could seem to be making a game out of outsmarting forces that would thwart forward progress. I couldn't understand what the big rush was to make a signal, and why it always seemed like we were in a hurry even when we were early. As you can see, there are plenty of differences here. One of Steve's great ideas is to hold hands and pray for removal of our character defects, together, using "we" instead of "I."

PRAYER*

Our Creator, we are now willing that You should have all of us, good and bad. We pray that You now remove from us every single defect of character which stands in the way of our usefulness to You and our fellows. Grant us strength, as we go out from here, to do Your bidding. Amen.

*Adapted from the Seventh Step Prayer *in Alcoholics Anonymous.*

7

AMENDS

By Angie

One day Steve suggested we have friends over to dinner. I hesitated, since I was projecting a pretty busy week. Sensing my hesitation, Steve said he would help me prepare dinner, so I agreed. When the day came, I got up, bought the groceries, went to my classes, and did other errands. I got home in the afternoon and began preparing dinner. He never came in to help. I went outside, where he was working on various projects, to ask things like, "Are you going to bring in greens from the garden for the salad?" I knew that he knew that I was inside preparing dinner.

I struggled with my resentment, trying to be grateful for my home, my husband, my friends—trying to minimize the situation and talk myself into thinking it was not that important. I tried to look at my part by asking myself how I could avoid that kind of disappointment in the future. I concluded that the next time he said he would help me with something like that, I would not believe him. It was just about time for our company to arrive, and he had not helped me. He had, in fact, forfeited some of my trust.

It was at that moment when he came into the kitchen and said, "I am aware that my words did not match my actions, and to make amends I will do all of the dishes for a week." He said he had gotten involved and carried away with his projects and did not feel good about not helping. I felt my heart melt. No more resentments, only renewed trust and appreciation! It felt good that he admitted his wrong, and even better that he had a concrete plan to make it right. This was a smart move and definitely beneficial for our relationship. This is also a good example of the power of amends as resentment destroyers.

It is important to note that I believe the proper response when someone makes amends is thanks and praise. That will encourage the desired behavior much more than jumping in about what a jerk he or she was.

PRAYER

Dear God, please help me to be gracious and forgiving whenever my partner admits a mistake. Help me to always offer praise and appreciation freely.

Agreement, integrity, and trust
By Steve (his version of the same situation)

I told Angie I would help her prepare dinner for guests beginning at 4:30 p.m. I entered into an agreement. Then I got distracted and put something else ahead of my agreement. I was out-of-integrity. I broke my agreement. My words and actions did not match. I wandered into the kitchen at 5:20 p.m. as the dinner preparation was nearly complete. Now…what do I do with this? Make excuses, try to shift responsibility, go on the attack? Or am I willing to be accountable?

I went to Angie and said, "I am out-of-integrity. I made an agreement with you that I did not keep. To get back in integrity, I wish to perform a simple act of service for you. I will clean every dish in the sink for the week starting Sunday morning and through Saturday evening." Angie agreed, I fulfilled my commitment, and guess what happened (besides us having great sex)? Angie said that she felt her trust in me go way up. For me it reinforced that there are consequences to my decisions and actions, and that I need to stay awake.

PRAYER

Dear God, please help me to continue to see the importance of my partner not having a resentment as a form of enlightened self-interest. May I always be willing to see where I have been impatient, selfish, fearful, or demanding. Give me the grace to ask myself those four magic words: what is my part? And please, God, give me the courage to set right any wrongs I have done and to protect our precious relationship.

Personal inventory, more about the magic of admitting you are wrong
By Angie

One weekend we were out of town when I got really angry at Steve. This is a rare occasion. Actually, I was mad at him for being mad at me. After all of the adjustments I had made! Why couldn't he just love and accept me the way I am? I awoke at 4:00 or 5:00 in the morning crying. I felt so upset, and resolution did not seem imminent. What would I have done if I were at home? I would have called a mentor or a friend. The solution appeared to be divorce; after all, I was fine before I was with him anyway, wasn't I? I prayed for a solution. I could envision a form that I had used from a writing exercise. The all-important question came to my mind: what was my part? I did have to admit that he was right about one thing.

Then I wondered why I was so upset. What was it I thought he had said? What was I reacting to? Well, I thought he said that he had never had any fun with me. I knew that probably wasn't true, because he is a smart man and if that were true, why would he have married me? By the time we talked, I was able to start the conversation by saying, "You were right about one thing," which I of course specified. I was then able to verify with him what he had actually said. The conversation went well from that point on and we were in love again within a couple of hours.

I seriously doubt there would have been such a desirable result if I had not admitted my part up front. That tends to soften the other person. The conversation went much better than if I had started out with something rash and angry, like, "You jerk, I want a divorce." Also, I am certain that my "reality check" and listening worked a lot better than reacting to what I *thought* he had said.

PRAYER

Dear God, please help me to search within and honestly admit my part to myself and others. Give me the courage to tell the truth despite fear of what others will think of me. Help me to be sure I understand the situation before I react from fear and ego.

Would I rather be right, or happy? How important is it, really?

By Angie

One morning I was having a light conversation with my husband. Basically, I was asking a few questions regarding a clubhouse reservation he had asked me to make for a friend. He informed me that he found this aggravating, and that it was not my fault. He was just in a bad place and unprepared to deal with this.

I went to the gym feeling frustrated and resentful. I hate when people ask me to do things and then act as though I am a nuisance for asking for clarification about something they wanted me to do in the first place. Of course I am right—who would not be upset?

But what good does that do me?

While at the gym, I thought about how I was in the middle of writing this book and how right now I certainly did not want to spend time writing about how to have a good relationship. But the book is about how to practice spiritual principles in a relationship! Then I asked myself what I would tell someone else to do. Well, I could pray. And what I would pray for? I would pray to love Steve the way he needs to be loved. And what is that right now? What does he need? He just needs to be left alone.

So, was it more important for me to remain right or to be happy? And, how important was this event, really? Steve occasionally needs to be given some time. This is normally a very temporary thing. I am married to a wonderful man who owns his own stuff. At least he did not try to blame it on me. This required me to be patient, but I want everything taken care of *now*. After all, who can blame me for being so efficient?

PRAYER

Dear God, please relieve me of the bondage of self and allow me to step back and love my partner the way he or she needs to be loved. Help me to remember back to the time when I would have longed for nothing more than to be with this person. Thank you for answering my prayers.

8

FINANCES

{ *Our common welfare* }

By Angie

When Steve and I finally found each other I was so happy; I had finally felt the love I had longed for all of my life. We married March 30, 2003. It was about the happiest day of my life, right up there with my daughter being born in 1965, and celebrating one year of recovery in 1979. When we moved in together, our financial agreement was to split expenses. I was retired many years before Steve will be. Our agreement when I retired was that I would do whatever he wanted for vacation with him, and anything else I wanted to do on my own.

In the fall of 2005, I was on my way to Italy with a girlfriend. As I was leaving, Steve was sinking into depression. When I returned, we had a discussion. He was very depressed. He was also conflicted about his feelings of unfairness, as he felt that my money was mine to spend as I saw fit; however, his job had become a huge struggle. He feared he would have to make a career change, as he did not feel able to continue his job at the current pace. We talked about what we could do to help his situation, and agreed that he would reduce what he contributed toward our monthly expenses, temporarily.

His depression worsened, and by the day after Thanksgiving, he told me he did not know if he could be married. I was devastated. There was a lot I did not understand about clinical depression. I really didn't get it, until Steve came home one day and said that someone in one of his men's groups had committed suicide; he was a teacher and had left a note saying he just could not grade the papers. Then I got how serious it was. Steve went on leave from his job for several months.

Gradually, he got better. We worked through the difficult period and emerged with a greater level of intimacy. I have felt secure within the relationship again for several years now, and he has been working part-time for a few of those years. Our marriage is great. After Steve got better, our financial arrangement would occasionally bug me. After all, if I were a real woman, I would have a man paying *my* rent (see "Space vs. Togetherness"). I finally had an "aha" moment where I got it. I was not doing it for him; I was doing it for him for *us*. Our marriage is better than ever. He is a better partner, more available, not to mention happier and healthier. Also, if he is able to retire earlier or travel more, it adds to the quality of *our* life. So, what is good for him is good for us, and of course, good for me.

Money, property, besiege

By Steve

When I was a kid, the emotional tide in my family home soared and crashed on the wings of financial prosperity or scarcity. When my father won the bid on a big contracting job, champagne corks would fly and we were soon on our way to a great vacation. When the tide inevitably turned, things got dark and everyone went to their separate corners to brood, occasionally taking time to sling hurtful arrows of recrimination.

My weekly allowances ended when I was twelve as my father began the slow, ugly process of exiting the family home, and eventually, my life, altogether. As a young boy, I always seemed drawn to find ways to make money, whether it was wheeling my wagon full of iced soda to a construction site, collecting newspapers to recycle, shoveling snow, or mowing lawns. I remember experiencing a sense of pride and accomplishment that was empowering when I bought my first Schwinn ten-speed bike.

I discovered that money provided independence. It instantly expanded my freedom to explore. I rode that bike from Levittown to Montauk Point, Long Island. Next I was purchasing my own car and starting a new life in California.

There were times of scarcity when I had to recycle bottles to get a meal. This motivated me to get an education. I hated the sense of powerlessness and vulnerability that came with poverty. And I certainly did not want to be financially and therefore emotionally dependent ever again. The drive was on to become a homeowner. It so happened that my girlfriend shared this goal, and we joined forces to purchase a home in Southern California. We got married a month later.

At the time, I incorrectly assumed that my new wife shared the goal of being able to consistently pay the mortgage and set some money aside for extras, such as travel and an occasional new car. Over time, however, it became clear that we were sinking—and not just financially. We had never discussed and come to agreement about our financial goals. We had never even had a meeting of our hearts regarding having children, or about our spiritual values. Ultimately, waking up to the reality of our grave and numerous areas of incompatibility sent shivers up my spine. Upon dissolution of that marriage, the drive was again on to be utterly self-reliant.

Fast-forward fifteen-plus years to the opportunity to step into partnership with Angie; I'll never forget the conversation we had on the sprawling lawn of the retreat center, where we discussed our fears around losing financial autonomy within a marriage. That is when it came to me: we don't have to handle money (or anything else) the way everybody or anyone else does it (or says it should be done). We can make our own rules! We are the only two architects of this relationship we are building. We made a decision to let go of old ideas and programming about how things "should" be.

We could pool together money to cover our joint living expenses however we pleased, and keep other money separate. An essential guideline is that if either of us starts to feel even a twinge of resentment, or that something isn't fair, we speak up immediately and work to resolve it. That's what we have been doing and it has been working well now for many years.

It's working because we both truly want our relationship to work. No other agenda comes before us wanting this to work. We both bring great forces to this common purpose: honesty, open-mindedness, willingness, creativity, rational thought, and the wise counsel of trusted advisers who have had specific experience with any area of difficulty that might arise.

9

WHEN PRINCE CHARMING SCREWS UP

{ *We don't leave no matter what* }

By Angie

In a previous topic ("Finances: Our common welfare") I described some of my feelings about Steve's depression and the point at which he said he did not know if he could be married. I am not proud about my initial reaction. It felt akin to panic: *I could get seriously hurt here, so I need to act first, and NOW!* He had punctured the balloon of my "happily ever after." Thoughts came up like, "Well, I was fine before we got together and I can be fine again without him." My first thoughts were of immediate separation. How could he do this to me? Looking back, I see it all came from ego and self-centered defensiveness.

Steve and I had been going to a couples meeting since our early dating days. I instinctively called a woman from that group. She gave me words of wisdom. She said, "You will always reach the place in a relationship where you are right now, the point where you want to leave. It may be different problems, but it will be the same place." She said that she wanted to be old and married, and the only way to do that was to hang in through the hard times and not leave. I also remembered other couples in the meetings expressing their commitment by saying, "We just don't leave no matter what." In addition, a wise and experienced friend had once told me that marriage was like a long railroad track; once in a while you go through some rough track, but if you stay on course it gets smooth again.

I am so grateful that I did hang in there, and that together we have experienced a life that is truly beyond my wildest dreams. We love and support one another and revel in giving service to others.

I do not mean to imply that there are not some relationships that have good reasons for ending, and I don't pretend to know what other people should do. I am only sharing my own experience and gratitude. I firmly believe that ours is a relationship meant to stay together and serve God.

DARK NIGHT OF THE SOUL AND
THE FOUR R's OF RELATIONSHIP

By Steve

Depression didn't usually give a lot of warning or explanation. I had done these emotional E-ticket rides through hell many times solo. I would batten down the hatches and ride out the storm. I kept the world at arm's length. Heaven help anyone who got in my way.

But now how could I go through this with someone at my side? I felt the walls closing in. Closeness made my skin crawl. I was feeling both territorial and terrified, whipsawing between lashing out and withdrawing. I felt myself sinking into an abyss.

In the past my strategy was to simply allow time to pass while not expecting too much from myself. But something was seriously wrong here. Time was passing and it kept getting worse. Several weeks in, it was so bad that I couldn't imagine it getting any worse. Then it got worse!

The harder I struggled to sort it out, uncover the problem, and find a solution, the more tangled up I got. Now what? I was left with nothing left to do but examine everything:

Could I continue to live in the city on concrete?

Could I keep showing up to my intense job?

Could I stay married?

When I took the risk of sharing honestly with Angie where I was, it was unsettling for her to say the least. We faced the task of negotiating our differing togetherness and solitude needs. We each had to do a lot of stretching to try to meet the other half way. There were times of utter disconnect and hopelessness. How fortuitous that at exactly the right time, a client shared with me something she had just learned in a workshop—that every relationship goes through the four R's, as follows:

The Four R's of Relationship

Romance—it's all good, gaga eyes, he or she can do no wrong, each person is putting his or her best foot forward.

Reality—over time, as you feel more comfortable, the warts are allowed to slowly start showing, and you see aspects of the other and yourself that are distasteful.

Rethinking—it's natural to think, "hmmm…is this relationship with this person what I really want? Is it worth the effort? Can I do better?"

Recommitment—ultimately all successful relationships involve both people making a decision to recommit to the relationship and then behaviorally demonstrating through words and actions the honoring of that commitment.

What a relief! What I was going through was a natural part of the process. There was a real possibility that recommitment could be just around the corner.

The wisdom of some indigenous cultures embraces decisions made by the coming together of 1) Right thinking, 2) Right timing, 3) Right position, and 4) Right action. Because my thinking was not right, I was not in position (spiritually, emotionally, or mentally), and, therefore, the timing was not right to make a big decision. The right action was no action. Breathe, pray, wait, trust, then repeat.

I am so grateful I did not act impulsively and make a decision I would later regret. I am glad I/we could tolerate sitting in the not-knowing, that unresolved place, and trust that more would be revealed and that the right answers would come.

THE END. AND NOW, FINALLY, THEY LIVED HAPPILY EVER AFTER.

No! Marriage is enhanced by action and more action—please read on!

PART III

Positive Action:
Nurturing the Garden

1

COMMUNICATION

{ *What I heard you say is…* }

By Angie

One evening I was sitting on the couch when Steve walked in and asked, "Did you eat all the puddings already?" I responded, "It's not like I ate them in one sitting. There were four puddings. I ate one per day. You had three pudding opportunities. And, what I heard you say is 'comma, you big fat pig.'" Steve looked shocked, as he was just wondering where the puddings were.

A couple of weeks later, we were driving down the street when I asked, "Honey, did you know there was a stop sign back there?" He said, "What I heard you say is, 'you jerk, don't you know how to drive?'"

Now we laugh about this, but it has become a useful communication tool to mirror back what we think we heard. Sometimes I can have a knee-jerk reaction to something because I am unconsciously and emotionally misinterpreting the comment according to my own issues and sensitivities. This technique helps to clarify the intent of the statement and to pave the way toward non-defensive communication. It can also introduce a healthy dose of humor into a discussion and help to ease tension.

EXERCISE

When your partner says something you find hurtful, try verifying what you think you heard before reacting.

On a scale of one to ten
By Steve

Here they come again, the holidays. For some a source of enduring joy; for others a source of dread, anxiety, and an urge to head for the hills, which is exactly what I used to do—go skiing.

As our third Christmas together approached, we found ourselves delicately stepping around the question of what we would do for Christmas Eve. I only knew that I wanted to do whatever I wanted to do. I just didn't know exactly what that was yet.

Using the past for reference only confused matters. I'd had a wide range of experiences. My gramps had died on December 21, when I was fourteen years old, which always seemed to color the holidays. Some of my memories were of being alone in a hotel room on a ski mountain, trying to escape my grief. Then there were my happier recollections, of singing Christmas carols in church with tears of joy running down my cheeks. As I wandered aimlessly through a maze of options in my head, Angie was able to communicate clearly what she wanted. She simply wanted to share a nice dinner with her daughter and husband on Christmas Eve. She had indicated that Christmas Eve had been a very special time that she and her daughter spent with her mother, who had died right before our first Christmas together.

I sensed that Angie and her daughter still had some distress around Christmas, but I didn't really get it until I had a moment of clarity. I asked Angie, "On a scale of one to ten, where would you rate the importance of this to you?" Without hesitation Angie shot back, "A ten." Meanwhile, I determined that holding on to my right to call the shots for Christmas Eve was only a three.

I instantly felt the relief of moving from struggle to settlement. Of course I would want my wonderful bride to have her heart's desire. I felt my need to maneuver to get my way fall away completely, leaving me with the vivid realization that I had held a narrow understanding of what true freedom is. My view had now expanded to include the freedom from living with an unsolved dilemma and the freedom from being in a power struggle to try to get something that wasn't even all that important to me.

Angie also reported feeling great relief. She had been frustrated from trying to 1) find a "new normal" after the loss of her mother, and 2) create a nice holiday with her daughter, who also had suffered greatly from the loss of her grandmother. Given the importance of the holiday for them, she vaguely sensed that I was being difficult. However, she had been unable to identify the feelings until my question clarified the issue. She expressed much gratitude and increased respect over my "surrender." I like it when that happens. In addition, we now have had many pleasant Christmas Eves.

Turning to this "scale of one to ten" has been a useful tool and has saved us a lot of unnecessary grief. For those issues where there is a distinct difference between our ratings, this tool has made compromise so much easier.

EXERCISE

The next time you and your partner are having a discussion regarding an issue, try honestly rating how important it is to each of you on a scale of one to ten.

> We have a set of questions that we find it helpful to ask ourselves before reacting to what could be a misunderstanding. We keep this posted on our refrigerator.
>
> • Do you and your partner have different needs around this issue? Are you sure you know what your partner's needs are? Can you ask before you react?
>
> • Is it possible that you have misinterpreted words or actions? Can you ask for clarification?
>
> • Does your partner have other stressors that you are not aware of?
>
> • Is it possible that your partner does not have all the facts?
>
> • Would your partner be as angry as you are if the situation were reversed?
>
> • Is it possible that this issue is much more important to your partner than you realize?
>
> • Bearing in mind that your partner's response may depend upon your attitude when you open the conversation, think carefully about how you want to start. How would you want to be approached?

What we hold sacred: five languages of love
By Steve

Something wasn't right. I felt deep love for Angie, and thought I was expressing it to her, but it seemed like she just was not feeling it. I was communicating my love in my language, not hers. Now when I mentor men who are in relationships, I find it helpful to encourage them to find out what makes their partners feel loved.

How do you communicate your love to your partner? How does your partner communicate love to you? In his book *The 5 Love Languages: The Secret to Love that Lasts*, Dr. Gary Chapman identifies five languages of love. How would you arrange the five languages of love from most to least important?

1. Acts of service

2. Quality time

3. Physical touch

4. Words of affirmation

5. Receiving gifts

The above is my order. I later learned that Angie had a different order:

1. Physical touch

2. Words of affirmation

3. Quality time

4. Acts of service

5. Receiving gifts

In fact, the point of this section on communication is to embrace open dialogue, and it is also of value here to remember: an ounce of "don't say it" is worth a pound of "didn't mean it." We can say what we mean, mean what we say, and not say it mean. We have shared some of what we have learned that has worked for us. We urge you to experiment in finding what works for you, whether it is through mirroring what you hear, rating issues, or simply asking questions (rather than assuming you already know).

EXERCISE

Examine for yourself what actions make you feel loved. Ask your partner to rank, in order of importance, the five languages of love, and to elaborate on what behaviors make him or her feel loved. Then communicate your discoveries about yourself to your partner. You may find some surprises, along with some useful information.

2

INTIMACY BUILDERS

{ *Four gateways to intimacy*
(weekly relationship inventory meeting) }

By Steve

A ngie and I were up in Portland, Oregon having breakfast with some friends when the topic turned to their weekly meeting with each other. They used it as a "check-in," a time to share how their week went and address any unresolved issues. They could then begin the new week with a clean slate and an awareness of each other's intentions and challenges.

Angie and I agreed that this was a great thing to add to our relationship. While waiting in the airport for our trip home, I came up with the following format for our weekly meeting, which consists of us each taking our turn in four sharing rounds:

First Round: Check-in

a) What am I feeling here and now?

b) What are my personal highs and lows of this past week?

Second Round: Accountability

a) Am I in integrity with my declared intentions with myself and others?

b) What needs to happen to be back in integrity?

Third Round: Manifestation

a) What am I intending for this coming week?

b) What are my challenges and personal stretches for the coming week?

c) What are five things I can do for my partner this week?

Fourth Round: Gratitude

a) Acknowledgement of blessings and gratitude for this encounter, for the week, for my life, for our life together.

One side benefit is that this process provides a good opportunity to make requests or ask for what we want in a positive, constructive way, instead of when we are upset about something we wish our partner would do. I would like to point out here the importance of a request vs. a demand. I get the most positive response when I start with, "Would you be willing to…?" (as opposed to a complaint, criticism, or command).

We have our inventory meeting on Sunday mornings and find it especially useful for those busy weeks when it seems we haven't really connected and loose ends or unanswered questions are left dangling. It also helps us to clarify our intentions for the coming week and to pre-pave the way for loving actions toward each other. We give ourselves the gift of each other's attention and sharing the language of the heart, where the heart speaks and the heart listens. You'll never guess how this meeting sometimes culminates….

Sharing

By Steve

As a curious young boy shining a flashlight beneath a homemade tent with my friend Nellie, I said, "I'll show you mine if you show me yours." Sharing between two people, it seems, is a natural instinct. We are social creatures. Great discovery and learning occurs through interaction, whether on the playground, in the workplace, or in the bedroom.

Although at times I can find great comfort in solitude, it is in communion with another or in the larger community that I thrive and gain life experiences that then enrich my alone time and provide grist for my writing. Yet sometimes sharing feels like the last thing in the world I want to do. I feel edgy, prickly, ill-equipped, unprepared, and vulnerable. It seems as though nothing good could possibly come from this agonizing exercise of "sharing." My natural instinct reverts to being a cave-dwelling animal: retreat, isolate, lick my wounds, and allow time to work its magic. Yet, it is the impulse of a herd animal to receive support and nurturing from others.

When the herd impulse does prevail, I am almost always better for it, now that I've developed enough trust in my own ability to know whom to trust. I've found that for me to be willing and for it to be wise to let down my armor and open my heart, I need to start with safe people and places. By safe people I mean those who do not tend to be judgmental or find it necessary to shut me down, overanalyze, or try to fix me when I start verbalizing my feelings. I've encountered people who are uncomfortable around raw grief, sadness, anger, fear—or pure joy, for that matter. This discomfort can prevent them from being present, when full presence is most essential for the sharing to flow.

Sharing must be welcomed in order to flow. Otherwise, I will intuitively shut it down, stuff it down. I got so good at this as a teenager that I didn't shed a tear when my grandfather died or my parents divorced. I rolled into my thirties utterly disconnected from my own heart and soul; it felt life-threatening to even start to go there. I remember sitting in a group of twenty people and being asked what I was feeling (because I was showing signs of agitation). I felt all the eyes in the room on me, and, with this seemingly simple inquiry hanging in the air, I just wanted to be able to answer the damned question and move on. But no matter how hard I tried, I had no idea, no sense of what I was feeling, other than numb. I was emotionally illiterate. I could not identify my feelings, much less know how to put them into words. It took work over a period of years to access deeply buried feelings and express them to appropriate people in appropriate settings. To begin sharing the contents of my heart and to reveal my secrets and innermost thoughts was a mark of great progress.

It is possible to go the other extreme of over-sharing, to leak toxicity into the container of a relationship that is dishonorable to self or others, has no usefulness, does not serve the relationship, or is a subtle or direct form of sabotage. There are the trivial, inconsequential, or neurotic ramblings better left unsaid, privately worked through (maybe in a journal) or shared with a mentor, confidante, sponsor, or spiritual adviser.

Overall, it is essential to acknowledge the importance of having the courage to share appropriately. Yes, we risk exposure and rejection. There can be the fear that no one will love us if they know who we really are. Yet most often spouses complain that their partners do not let them in; they feel isolated, lonely, and shut out. That is the opposite of feeling the intimacy and connectedness required for a relationship to thrive. Perhaps, in part, it is our very vulnerability that binds us together.

Listening

By Angie

I grew up in an Italian family. Gatherings were kind of like those portrayed in the movies where everyone talks loudly and excitedly, with large hand gestures, and all at the same time. It was considered very polite if you simply did not talk at the same time as another person.

Steve and I would have extended conversations long before we started dating. I think I talked way too much and probably interrupted a lot, most likely from nervousness. Also, Steve tends to speak more slowly than I do, and when he would finish a sentence and pause, I would sometimes think he was done. As time went by I became less nervous and would usually listen until he seemed to have told me whatever he wanted to say about a subject. Sometimes I would share a personal experience related to the topic. At other times, I would change the subject when I thought he had completed what he wanted to communicate to me. I did hear everything he said, and could repeat it back to you. Like I said, in my family, that would have been considered great listening.

I was surprised to learn that often Steve did not feel heard. I was sad when he said that made him feel lonely. I do know that sometimes I have trouble being fully present, in the here and now. (I am a great planner, you know, and always thinking ahead.) Steve is a wonderful listener. I can't explain it, but when he listens to someone it is as if he is giving a special gift to him or her—as if his depth of presence welcomes, invites, draws out, and holds a space for things to come out that would not otherwise be shared.

He shared with me some reflective questions and comments that I could use to help him feel heard. Then, he developed the "Helpful Hints That Support Intimacy" that we are sharing below. (Of course, I am not always able to practice all of these hints, but they are very useful guidelines on how I can continue to improve my listening skills.)

Helpful Hints That Support Intimacy

• Be fully present with mind, body, and spirit for your partner, and ask for this of your partner when you need it.

• Do what's needed to free yourself of any intruding distractions, whether internal or external.

• Trust that Spirit, yours and your partner's together, is bigger than any impermanent mental or emotional pain or fear.

• Be present for yourself as you are present for your partner; be present to what goes on internally for yourself as your partner expresses feelings or thoughts.

• Wait for an opportune time to share that won't derail your partner's process.

• See if you can keep any dialogue to here and now, vs. past. "Here with you right now, I'm feeling or I'm noticing or I'm sensing _____."

• If you feel your partner withdrawing at some level, check it out by asking, "Is there something calling or pushing you away right now?"

• If curious, inquire with your partner:

  • What's coming up for you right now?

  • Do you have a sense of what this is about?

  • What is this connecting with for you?

  • What's it like to say this out loud?

- Empathize: for example, "That sounds painful."

- Ask, "Is there anything that would be helpful for me to do or not do right now?"

- Ask, "Are you aware of what you need right now?"

- Before ending, ask, "Do you feel complete?"

- Now is a good time to debrief, share your experiences and blessings received from this encounter. Do you feel closer to your partner? Do you feel more trusted by or trusting in your partner? Do you feel honored to be included in his or her deep work?

- Is there a physical act of affection to be expressed? Is there something nurturing or fun you could partake in together now?

Ten questions game
By Steve

When I was a young person, one of the things to do with your new sweetie after a rousing round of spin the bottle was to play "Twenty Questions." It was a way to get to know someone quickly, depending on the quality of the questions and the honesty of the answers.

Angie and I, in keeping with our tradition of doing something different each New Year's Eve, planned a date at the ocean's edge at sunset, each with our list of questions. Since we already had quite a jump on this "inquiring minds" business, we decided to keep it at ten questions. It was interesting that Angie and I had a number of similar questions as well as similar answers to some of the questions.

To give you a better idea, here is a list of sample questions.

1. What is more important to you than anything else? Or, what is your greatest dream?

2. What are three aspirations for yourself before you die? Or, will you share your "before I die" list with me?

3. What three things would you like me to do for you? Or do more of?

4. What are your three biggest fears? Or, what is your greatest fear?

5. What is the biggest disappointment of your life? Or, what is your greatest regret?

6. Which of your accomplishments are you most proud of?

7. List at least three things you love about yourself.

8. What are three great things about our marriage/relationship?

9. What do you see as the greatest challenge(s) we face together?

10. Describe in detail your ideal day from start to finish.

11. Name five (or more) of the greatest events of your life.

12. Where do you see yourself ten years from now?

We had so much fun doing this. It felt intimate to have that kind of conversation, like when we were first dating. We had found that even though we had not been married very many years, our conversations had too often become dominated by the business of living, such as the plumbing, house painting, bills, etc.

3

REINFORCING THE POSITIVE

{ *Marriage journal, cherishing the good times* }

By Steve

I don't remember ever having a great memory. So when I began keeping a journal in 1976, it mostly consisted of noting the rock concerts, campouts, and parties I went to. Every now and then I'd write a page or two in more detail about what was going on around me and/or within me. One time I had nothing better to do, and I pulled out a journal from a prior year. Reading the entries, I got to relive the great times I enjoyed. I realized that without the journal, those experiences might have been lost forever, beyond the reach of my

recall. This caused me to want to keep journaling.

Shortly after Angie and I got married, I bought Angie a journal as a birthday gift and presented it to her when we were out for dinner. But in between the time I got the journal and when I gave it to Angie, the inspiration hit for it to be a "marriage journal." Besides, as Angie once said when we were dating, "I'll be the simple one; I'm not going to feel like I have to come up with weird stuff (meaning new and innovative things to try). That will be your job."

If one person can keep a journal, then why can't a couple? We would take turns making entries about our life together, expressing our gratitude for special moments and vacation highlights. Sometimes we would paste a comic strip, poem, or photo onto a page. We also started writing down the funny things that popped out of our mouths, especially those that made us laugh really hard.

The following February Angie thought to bring the journal with us to our annual couples retreat. One night we sat in bed reading the journal and laughing hysterically. We were now both hooked on the marriage journal idea. Some of the most hilarious moments we have shared would have been forgotten without the journal. Instead, we get to relive over and over again things that brought us great joy. It is one more way of helping us to focus on the good times.

A retreat? No, it's an advance!

Get out of the house, out of town, out of routine, offline, unplugged, and distraction-free. Slow down, find a beautiful place, gaze into each other's eyes, and enjoy a getaway—for the weekend if possible.

As comfortable as a home can be, it is not always that easy to "laze on a Sunday afternoon." There is the phone, the dishes, the kids or grandkids, the pets, the yard, the honey-do list, email, requests, and "gottas" that spire out of the floorboards or stalagmite from the ceiling demanding attention. The best of intentions to kick back, lock the bedroom door for some afternoon delight, or otherwise connect with your life partner, get pushed aside. Again.

I remember having a hellacious toothache once. I called up the dentist and got an appointment as soon as possible. I was highly motivated to keep that appointment. Let's see, should I write it in my appointment book in pencil or pen? How likely do you think it would have been for me to allow something to stand in the way of me showing up at the appointed time and place? I've observed a strange but common occurrence: many people harness great energy to show up for things that they will admit are not vital or even important, yet when it comes to something as vital as our relationship, complacency can win out. We can regularly attend to non-important activities while our relationship is dying of neglect. I became aware that I could easily do a year's worth of work in ten months, but not twelve. In other words, if I didn't get off of the concrete and beneath the trees, to the mountains or the sea for a decent chunk of time, I began to suffer and so did my work and my relationship. I also became aware that I loved the change of seasons and delighted in the variety of sights, sounds, textures, fragrances, and personalities of the four seasons.

These treats could easily pass me by if I was too immersed in my work and stuck in the city. For this reason, Angie and I started giving ourselves the gift of a quarterly retreat to a beautiful, restful, or engaging place. It's a chance to be released from demands and distractions, and to give to ourselves and our union the gifts of being present, slowing down, and sharing our love. Surprising delights await when we co-create a ratcheted-down pace, change of scenery, and freedom from the to-do list.

There is one thing a lot of struggling couples have in common: they can't remember the last time they got away for a long weekend together—alone. I've also noticed that a getaway free of distractions can feel threatening to a coupleship in trouble. It can be like turning a microscope on a wound—great if you want to see what needs healing, terrible if you'd just as soon look the other way and hope it magically remedies itself.

PRAYER

God, please help us to take time apart from our busy lives to honor our partnership and give our full attention to the blessings of our union. May we make the time, even if it is only a one-day retreat, to go for a hike, sit at the beach, or take a day trip someplace where we can be alone. Help us to be willing to face being alone together, away from our daily responsibilities, to renew ourselves and our direction as a couple so that we may emerge refreshed and better able to serve You.

Building and honoring the container

> **Contain**: to keep within limits; to prevent (as an enemy or opponent) from advancing or making a successful attack; to have within; hold, comprise, include, enclose, to restrain oneself.*

It was an alien concept when I first heard a relationship described as a container. What two people bring to the container of their relationship will determine the quality, nature, and possibilities for the relationship. If both bring honesty and compassion, it will be an honest and compassionate vessel capable of surviving rough seas. If one or both bring deception, judgment, and selfishness, it will create an unpleasant union with low life expectancy.

I AM RESPONSIBLE FOR

• What I bring to the container of my relationship.

• Staying awake to what is going on in the container.

• Bringing solutions to challenges experienced in the relationship, which yields much more desirable outcomes than complaining, defending, or stubbornly clinging to my position.

• Not polluting the container with toxic words, attitudes, or actions.

By permission. From Merriam-Webster's Collegiate Dictionary, 11th Edition©2011 by Merriam-Webster, Incorporated (www.merriam-webster.com).

- Keeping in what belongs in the container and keeping out what does not belong. This means:

  - I don't complain about my spouse to anyone other than my spouse and my spiritual adviser.

  - I don't join in with anyone talking negatively about my spouse.

  - I don't share intimate details about my marriage outside the marriage.

  - All erotic energy is sacredly contained in the relationship and is not carelessly shared elsewhere.

IT ALSO MEANS

- Valuing the container and allowing it to grow strong.

- Remaining alert and responsive to anything that could compromise it.

- Celebrating with gratitude that I get to be in a quality partnership.

Vitamin G, the gratitude list

Many years ago, while I was complaining about my life, a man challenged me to go home that night and write down ten things for which I was grateful. Sadly, I could not do it. I had grown virtually incapable of experiencing gratitude. My gratitude muscle had atrophied from lack of use. Nothing was ever enough. I usually had one eye trained on "next" and the other on "more." I remember drinking my first beer from a six-pack and thinking, "Damn, now I only have five left." I have to tell you, I hate not being good at something, especially if it seems like it should be simple. So I began a practice of writing down things for which I am grateful. Something remarkable happened. A couple of years later as a part of a retreat exercise, we were invited to write down one hundred things we are grateful for, and I was able to do it!

In many of my marital counseling sessions, it would become apparent that both parties had totally lost sight of what attracted them to their partner in the first place. If I focus on what is lacking in my partner, I will probably be able to find something. A gratitude list is especially useful in a relationship.

One day very early in our dating, Angie and I both spontaneously, separately, unknowingly, and almost simultaneously, wrote a list of "what I like about you," as she explained in the section "My Magic Magnifying Mind." We have continued to exchange annual lists, and usually paste them into our marriage journal. When we hit periods of discontent, it is human to blame our mood on the other person. That is a good time to get out those lists and reflect on them. It's also a good time to make a new gratitude list or keep a gratitude journal for a while.

I have a choice of an "attitude of gratitude" or a "litany of pity me."

Attitude power

> **Attitude**: a posture, a mental position with regard to a fact or state, a feeling or emotion toward a fact or state.*

It had never occurred to me what a pivotal influence my attitude held over my mental and emotional state. It determines how I approach the world and relationships, how I make decisions, how I create my life, and whether I have a positive or negative experience.

What is my attitude toward my partner today? What is my attitude toward a healthy lifestyle? Is my attitude along the lines of "Poor me, it's not fair. Other people can be in and enjoy a relationship, yet I can't seem to"? Do I see my relationship, or my being alone right now, as a burden or a blessing? A curse or a gift? A problem or an opportunity? Our attitude can be static and fixed, or it can be dynamic and ever-changing. Attitude can change by itself, or we can make a conscious decision to change our attitude. Am I willing to make certain adjustments? What are they?

*By permission. From Merriam-Webster's Collegiate® Dictionary, 11th Edition©2011 by Merriam-Webster, Incorporated (www.merriam-webster.com).

Who is in charge of what goes on in your mind? Somebody else, or is that somebody you?

My acceptance of responsibility for my attitude is empowering. My willingness to change or have my attitude changed will determine the quality of my life. For example, there is a fine line between boredom and serenity, between envy and admiration, and between anxiety and excitement; the difference comes down to attitude.

Am I willing to go to any length, to any depth, to line up my attitude with what I say I want? Am I truly prepared to receive what I say I want? What attitude shall I bring to my life and my relationship, or to setting out to attract a partner?

EXERCISE

Make a list of all the characteristics or behaviors that you want your partner (or future partner) to demonstrate. Post that list. Then work on practicing or developing those traits/behaviors yourself.

4

INSPIRATIONS FROM STEVE'S
CLINICAL PRACTICE

{ *Spiritual connection vs.*
emotional dependency }

By Steve

I have always been fascinated by what makes people tick and what makes relationships thrive or fail. I started my education and training to become a licensed marriage and family therapist in 1990. I have worked in a community counseling center, private practice, with public agencies such as children's services, an emergency psychiatric unit, and now a large health-care provider. One day I happened to be reflecting on relationships—those I had been in, as well as the many I had observed over the years. I had also recently had an experience where I had been overcome by powerful, unpleasant emotions, but turned my attention to spiritual principles I had been taught and instantly felt a huge shift and became emotionally free.

I became aware that the frustrating, painful, and unfulfilling relationships seemed to be based more on emotional dependency, while the easy-flowing, fun relationships had, at their foundation, more of a spiritual connection. I started to note the stark contrast between these two types of relationships and all the attendant qualities of each:

Spiritual Connection to Another	Emotional Dependency on Another
In the moment, here and now	Past and/or future oriented
Spontaneous, free-flowing	Involves attempts to control, be taken care of
Not manageable by human power A gift from Spirit?	Involves conscious/unconscious attempts by ego to manage outcome
Free of unrealistic expectations	Unrealistic expectations, spoken and/or unspoken
Love-based, joy-producing	Fear-based, misery-producing
Principles before personalities	Personalities before principles
Enhancing to spiritual condition	Worsening to spiritual condition
Abundance-based (plenty to go around)	Scarcity-based (if you win, I lose)
Horizontal relationship between equals: adult-to-adult interactions	Vertical relationship: one assumes role of superior, the other role of inferior
Synergy: the sum is greater than parts	Relationship diminishes those in it
Sustainable indefinitely	Unsustainable over time
Light-expanding, energy-brightening	Light-dimming, energy-depleting
Unlimited potential for expanded consciousness and growth	Unlimited potential for constricted consciousness and "stuckness"

Helpful ground rules

I have used the following list as basic "ground rules" for couples when working to achieve more harmony in a relationship:

WAYS TO A MORE PEACEFUL RELATIONSHIP

1. Be patient with yourself and each other. We are all a work in progress.

2. You have begun a process that involves change and requires acceptance and honesty.

3. Celebrate your successes; keep a sense of humor for your temporary setbacks.

4. Remember that both people have individual experiences, wounds, needs, and ways of seeing and reacting to the world. Having differences doesn't mean one person is right and the other wrong. Sometimes all you can do is agree to disagree.

5. Treat and talk to each other and yourself with respect.

6. Tell the truth. Say what you mean, mean what you say, but don't say it mean. Honesty without compassion can be brutality.

7. Really listen and hear each other out. Give what you want to get—an open mind, an open heart.

8. Own your own position and feelings. Don't get caught in the painful, dead-end trap of blame, pointing the finger. Sentences that begin with "You" immediately put people on the defensive.

9. Stay in the present moment; don't use the past to attack.

10. Avoid unhelpful terms like "you always. . ." and "you never…"; they are indictments, and derail useful dialogue.

continued on page 110

11. Anger is useful in that it tells us something is wrong. It is vital to be able to express anger appropriately and non-violently and let it go. Be alert to the mistake sometimes made of holding on to our anger as a way to avoid dealing with the hurt.

12. Remember we are powerless over other people's feelings, thoughts, attitudes, and actions. Trying to control another person is disrespectful (and exhausting). It is a full-time job observing our own thoughts and progressing toward constructive, rather than destructive, attitudes and actions.

13. Forgiveness doesn't mean you approve of the behavior or that it is acceptable for it to be repeated, it means that you are letting go of the hurt and taking responsibility for healing it and not putting yourself in the position to be hurt again. Forgiving isn't forgetting, it's being able to remember without bitterness.

14. Know your limits and communicate them clearly along with the consequences. Examples: "Ouch, it is hurtful hearing you say those words to me. I refuse to be talked to that way. If it continues, I will need to question whether being in a relationship with you is in my best interest." "If you start using drugs again you will have to find another place to live immediately."

Rocking the coupleship (with sex and healthy risk-taking)

The $64,000 question—actually, allowing for inflation, the $1,000,000 question—is: how and why does the passion drain out of some relationships? Is it preventable?

As relationships mature, it is not unusual for the passion enjoyed in the beginning years to mellow as two people "settle in" together. Instead of anticipation of dates for the upcoming weekend, we are now living together. Instead of only doing fun things together, we are now attending to the business of living, managing household/kids together. Instead of spending a limited amount of time together, we are now together full-time. And what if there is disagreement on how to meet a challenge or solve a problem? Life can have a way of closing in on and swallowing up the time and energy formerly devoted to expressing passion for each other and enjoying physical intimacy. Many couples have to make extra effort to stay awake, set time aside—literally schedule getaway weekends, a day, or even half-day, to snuggle, take a romantic walk, or share a special meal together. And yet setting aside these times seems essential in order to keep passion alive.

TRADITIONS AND
NEW RENDITIONS

By Steve

In my old life, when I was drinking and single, I had certain habits, rituals, and traditions. Halloween was usually the kick-off season for depression that deepened with shorter days. The emotional baggage I carried around the Christmas holidays often led to morbid reflection, feeling sorry for myself, and wanting to isolate. I would go up to Mammoth Lakes, ski all day, and drink myself into a stupor at night.

Of course, a lot of things changed when I got into recovery. Then when Angie and I came together as a couple, we had the opportunity to preserve or purge our individual traditions, while co-creating new traditions just for us. Angie's mother had died when we were first dating, so together we faced the process of "finding a new normal." We gingerly embraced a new life, breaking free from feeling bound to the past.

For example, one of the new traditions we share together is to spend New Year's Eve each year doing something completely different. Then, shortly after the new year has begun, we have a small party to share food and a ritual with friends. We get together and write lists of what we want to say "good-bye" to from the past year, then we gather around a fire chanting "good riddance" phrases while each list goes up in smoke. We then write ourselves letters stating our visions of what we would like to manifest during the upcoming year. (Angie holds those sealed letters for a year, and then mails them to our friends along with an invitation for the next year's gathering.) Then we all share about the past year and our visions for the new year.

Angie and I are never at a loss as to what to do for Valentine's Day, as we always spend it at our annual couples retreat. We eagerly anticipate celebrating our wedding anniversary in March. In May, I am usually off to Yosemite for some solo renewal time in nature. We look forward to free outdoor summer concerts and annual campouts. In addition, we schedule visits to our out-of-state families, and a fall retreat. We also try to go to at least one place we have not been each year. We find joy in and savor the blessings of each season, for example the arrival of the autumn soup season.

These are a few of our traditions, and we hope they will encourage you to create some of your own.

EXERCISE

Take some time to reflect on your traditions as a couple. How well have you balanced your personal preferences, family needs, and obligations? What truly brings you joy? Is there anything you would like to add to your life? Are you both comfortable with the compromises you have made? Is there anything that would help to compensate for some of the compromises? What does each of you wish to bring into your life over the next twelve months?

POWER OF PRAYER AND MEDITATION

{ *Moving it from an individual practice into the relationship* }

By Steve

I was a natural-born cynic and self-professed skeptic. It took many years and a lot of hard knocks before I got willing to revisit the practice of prayer. As a child, I had to memorize and recite prayers. As an adolescent, I rebelled against practices that I felt had no meaning to me at that time.

Besides, to whom was I praying? I had lost conscious contact with a "higher power." I had taken on distorted and less-than-useful images of God. If God truly did see and know all, then I figured I was screwed. I kept a low profile, so God wouldn't pinpoint my location. My strategy became: if I don't bother God, hopefully God won't bother me. I didn't want to call attention to myself. Better to stay below the radar.

Today prayer and meditation play an integral part of my life, and of our relationship. In fact, before we share a meal, we touch foreheads and whoever feels inspired softly speaks a few words of gratitude for the food we are about to enjoy and any other blessings. We hold hands and pray before we pull out of the driveway to travel. Prayer has been especially valuable when we're about to discuss a touchy topic. I can feel tension drain and walls come down when we join in prayer.

The pivotal role of prayer in our lives is sprinkled throughout our story and vignettes. Prayer and meditation were instrumental in preparing both Angie and me to be in union with one another, and in our actual coming together. It is through constant practice and application of spiritual tools that we are happily married.

In closing I want to share that I no longer see prayer as an opportunity for me to try to change God's mind. I do see meditation as an opportunity for God to change my mind.

REFLECTION

Have you ever meditated with your partner? Have you ever found a beautiful, tranquil setting and simply sat quietly together, contemplatively?

PART IV

Keeping the "I" in Marriage

(When "for Me" = "for Us")

I hold this to be the highest task of a bond
between two people; that each should
stand guard over the solitude of the other.

For, if it lies in the nature of indifference and
of the crowd to recognize no solitude, then love and
friendship are there for the purpose of continually
providing the opportunity for solitude.

And only those are the true sharings which
rhythmically interrupt periods of deep isolation.

A togetherness between two people is an impossibility,
and where it seems, nevertheless to exist, it is but a
narrowing, a reciprocal against which robs either party
or both of their fullest freedom and development.

But, once the realization is accepted that even
between the closest human beings infinite distance
continues to exist, a wonderful living side by side can
grow up, if...they succeed in loving the distance between
them, which makes it possible for each to see the other
whole and against a wide sky.

An excerpt from: *On Love and Other Difficulties* by Rainer Maria Rilke

1

BACKGROUND

{ *Practicing self-care* }

By Angie

In Part One we wrote about our paths as individuals becoming ready and willing to be in partnership with another human being—what it was like, what happened to change us, and how we got together. In Part Two we described how we survived bumps in the road in order to stay together. In Part Three we shared positive steps to enhance the relationship and work together as a couple.

And now can't we live "happily ever after" like in the fairy tales? Yes, but not exactly. We are happy. We are together. We are in love with each other, and we love our lives. Yet we have also come full circle back to where we as individuals need to continue essential self-care for the benefit of the relationship as a whole. I love the analogy of an airplane scenario, where we are cautioned to put on our own oxygen masks before helping others. What do we need for survival and feeding of our own soul? For each person it may be different. For some it might mean participating in their religious community, charitable organizations, hobbies, or anything they feel passionate about. For those of us in recovery it means working our own programs to ensure ongoing freedom from life-threatening addiction and destructive compulsive behaviors.

Overview of the recovery process

What do we mean by recovery and the associated terms we have used? We will provide some brief explanations, primarily for the benefit of those readers who may not be familiar with twelve-step programs. These are our opinions, based upon our experience and understanding.

If our priority is our own ongoing recovery, we may need to take time apart from our partner to help others to find recovery. This is referred to as sponsorship, which we will expand upon later. We also think it is important to rely on the God of our understanding, rather than to make our partner our higher power, which we will also talk more about. We also need to go to twelve-step meetings. People have asked, "Why do you still have to go to those meetings?" Sometimes, if appropriate, I respond, "Why do you still go to church?" Then they understand.

In addition, we need to be honest and authentic. This requires a high level of trust and respect for each other's individuality. Neither Steve nor I want to have "white-knuckled abstinence" from our addictive behavior. We both seek what might be called a higher level of recovery, sometimes referred to as "emotional sobriety" (from whatever manifestation of addiction or compulsive behavior).

We have made reference to twelve-step recovery programs and spiritual principles. What do these things mean? First, for anyone unfamiliar, I will briefly summarize and roughly paraphrase the Twelve Steps of recovery, and then we will illustrate examples of spiritual principles. For the exact language of the steps, please refer to any of the official twelve-step program literature, the basic "mother" text being found in the book entitled, *Alcoholics Anonymous*, which is lovingly referred to as "the Big Book." These steps appear in some version in all twelve-step programs.

In Step One we admit that we are powerless over a substance, obsession/compulsion, or behavior, and that our lives are unmanageable. In Step Two we come to believe that a power greater than ourselves can restore us to sanity. In Step Three we turn our will and lives over to that power (i.e., God as we understand God). In Step Four we take a fearless and thorough moral inventory of ourselves, and in Step Five we share that inventory (admitting our wrongs to God, ourselves, and another human being). In Steps Six and Seven we become ready to have God remove all of our defects of character and humbly ask Him to remove these shortcomings. In Steps Eight and Nine, we make a list of all persons we had harmed, become willing to make amends, and do so wherever possible, except where others would be harmed. In Step Ten, we continue to take personal inventory, and when we are wrong, we admit it promptly. In Step Eleven, we seek through prayer and meditation to improve our conscious contact with the God of our understanding, praying only for knowledge of His will for us and for the power to carry that out. Step Twelve says we have had a spiritual awakening as the result of these steps, and that we therefore try to carry the message to others and to practice these principles in all of our affairs.

This brings us to the question: what are "these principles"?

Spiritual principles of the Twelve Steps

By Steve

The Twelve Steps are principles, spiritual in their nature, which if practiced as a way of life can expel obsessions and enable the sufferer to become happily and usefully whole.*

I was taught that practicing these spiritual principles accesses spiritual law, which unleashes infinite spiritual power—a power greater than the spiritual malady that can underlie and manifest in addiction. But the visceral experiences I have had and continue to have with these principles are what keep the Twelve Steps alive in my being.

Step	Principle	Practicing the principle of the current step produces a result which then puts me in position to practice the principle of the subsequent step.
1	Acceptance	Fully conceding to my innermost self my powerlessness and unmanageability, that without help the dis-ease is too much for me, that nothing changes until I first accept the reality as it exists in this moment.
2	Needing others	It all started with Bill W reaching out to Dr. Bob, then a third member needing them both. I needed guidance because my main problem centered in my mind. I needed support because self could not overcome self.
3	Trust	True test: am I willing to be rigorously honest, not hold back? Ultimately mistrust has the power to kill me if it prevents me from trusting a trustworthy person who is in a position to help me.
4	Honesty	Step Four (personal inventory) will be fearful and shallow if Step Three (turning will and life over to care of a higher power) work is incomplete. Practicing honesty leads us to sharing, which is the principle of Step Five.
5	Sharing	Sharing the Fifth Step will uncover defects that block me and my relationships from the sunlight of the Spirit and keep me isolated. It reveals defects I will become willing to have removed. When I practice the principle of needing others, this puts another in a position to practice the principle of sharing and vice versa.
6	Willingness	Am I willing (under the conditions of this day) to have these uncovered defects lifted from me, if they stand in the way of relationship with self, others, and a power greater than self?

continued on page 123

*Paraphrased from *The Twelve Steps and Twelve Traditions* by Alcoholics Anonymous.

Step	Principle	Practicing the principle of the current step produces a result which then puts me in position to practice the principle of the subsequent step.
7	Humility	Having an accurate perception of self in relation to others and a power greater than self and others; honest desire to seek and do higher power's (HP's) will.
8	Forgiveness	It is not about forgetting the past (the real or perceived hurt), but being able to remember the past without bitterness. Forgiveness is a gift of emotional freedom we give ourselves through doing the work. Forgiving frees us to be able to give as before the hurt occurred.
9	Restitution	An act of restoring, setting right the wrongs done, becoming emotionally free of past.
10	Self-examination	Helps keep us in position to be conscious and make conscious contact.
11	Surrender	We cease fighting, join the winning side, and abandon ourselves to a HP. Meditation is about letting go, opening to receive; prayer isn't about trying to change HP's mind, but opening to allow HP to change my mind.
12	Love	For me, it simply was not possible to experience love, to truly extend and receive love until I surrendered and practiced the preceding principles.

I believe spiritual law got me into recovery for a purpose, and that my job is to remain open and willing to allow this purpose to continually manifest through practicing these principles.

Angie adds:

The principles have also been described in other ways. One, as Steve alluded to in his opening, is that they are the steps themselves. Bill Wilson, co-founder of Alcoholics Anonymous, wrote in the *AA Grapevine* (July 1953), "I had set down certain principles which, upon being counted, turned out to be twelve in number." Another explanation is that they are derived from the spiritual tenets of the Oxford Group, a spiritual organization that Bill W and Dr. Bob were members of before they formed what became known as Alcoholics Anonymous.

There is some variation in other interpretations and twelve-step literature as to the principles connected with each step. They are variously cited as

• Honesty (Step One)

• Hope (Step Two)

• Faith (Step Three)

• Courage and Integrity (Steps Four and Five)

• Willingness (Step Six)

• Humility (Step Seven)

• Self-discipline and Love for others (Steps Eight and Nine)

• Perseverance (Step Ten)

• Spiritual Awareness—Practicing Prayer and Meditation (Step Eleven)

• and Service (Step Twelve).

I have seen other iterations as well; however, there is usually some commonality.

Ironically, the biggest disagreement Steve and I had in writing this book was about treatment of spiritual principles. This is an example of how we can agree to disagree, each have his or her own voice, and in the larger picture still be on the same page (pun intended). Steve wanted to address the spiritual principles associated with each step as he was taught and personally experienced them, because we are sharing our own experience, rather than what may already be available elsewhere. I wanted to include the principles as they were presented in official literature, with which everyone may not be familiar. These are included merely as *examples* of spiritual principles (as opposed to a conclusion about which principle should be connected to each of the twelve steps). What matters is that we agree on the need to acknowledge the importance of spiritual principles, practice our own concept of each, be conscious of a higher power guiding our lives, and try to do the right thing.

An important note: *It is essential that we love and honor each other by allowing the other to work his or her own program of recovery, with his or her own higher power.*

My recovery program works best when I acknowledge my own wrongs and character defects, rather than pointing out Steve's. It is also best when I use "I" statements when I need to talk to him about how I feel about something. Furthermore, it is none of my business how he chooses to sponsor, what meetings he goes to, etc. For example, it is Steve's personal choice and belief that it is healthy for him to fast on occasion. For me, this would be counter-therapeutic for my psyche. Great, so I don't have to fast. I expressed my concerns about his fasting once (well, maybe twice), and then it became none of my business except to work on accepting and supporting his choices. After all, do I want him telling me what I should eat? You bet I don't. I often appreciate the value of his opinion or input, especially if I have sought advice from him, and vice versa. But after that, it is our mutual task (and maybe sometimes challenge) to respect and support each other's choices.

Stages of change
By Steve

Just as it took moving from total denial of my addiction to considering that I might have a problem, to preparing to do something about it, and finally taking the action—I went through a similar process of denial around what attitudes, beliefs, and defects of character of mine stood in the way of my participating in a desirable relationship.
If the stages of change had a voice they could be characterized by the following statements:

Preawareness Stage

"Leave me be; get off my back!"

"I do not see that I have a problem with compulsive behavior or substance abuse."

"I'm not adding to the problem in this relationship. If only she/he would do this or stop doing that."

"I am not interested in anybody's ideas or solutions."

Growing Awareness Stage

"If I don't address my addiction, my problems are going to just get worse.

"The writing is on the wall, and it is growing larger and more unavoidable."

"But there is still a part of me that clearly wants to be able to keep using/engaging in compulsive behavior."

"Maybe I am in fact contributing to some (or, say it isn't so, all) of what is making this relationship painful to participate in."

"I am growing more curious. Is there a better way? I may be willing to take action in the coming months."

"On Your Mark, Get Ready" Stage

"The distress I am experiencing is severe enough to motivate me to take action in the coming days."

"I know why I want to make changes, and I am exploring resources, developing an action plan, and forming a support system."

"I have some concern that my actions may not get the results I want." (Especially if there have been past failed attempts to remain free of abusive substances or behavior, or to be in a desirable relationship).

"I have some ideas about what I need to do differently now."

"Go!" Stage

"I am committed to making changes today, as demonstrated by my actions."

"I am taking actions each day that support my recovery and starve the disease of addiction."

"I am participating in the solution (which begins with owning my part in the problem) for my relationship challenges."

"I am beginning to learn and practice new ways of dealing with upsetting feelings."

"I am willing to receive support from others, rather than try to do it all on my own."

Early Recovery

"I am now clearly reaping the rewards of my efforts, and so it makes sense to continue to work all Twelve Steps of recovery."

"I am encouraged by the progress of how I am relating to others."

"I know my personal relapse risk factors and emotional triggers, and I have coping strategies that I am practicing and strengthening."

"I entertain no illusions that I will someday be able to successfully use my substance/addictive behavior or blame my unhappiness on a relationship or another person."

"I am connecting on a regular basis with people who are also committed to their recovery and participating in healthy and satisfying relationships."

Advanced Recovery

"I am now working smarter, not harder. Recovery truly is the easier, softer way."

"I am passing it on, thrilled to be useful to others, and am enjoying the spiritual fruits from having service to others as a part of my life."

"My life is in balance."

"I am whole and complete, independent of what others around me are doing or not doing."

"I have replaced as my chief motivator the 'stick' of pain, fear, and desperation, with the 'carrot' of long-term, contented, and useful recovery, which may or may not include a life partner."

What do you mean by spiritual path?

By Steve

It all began with experiencing a *spiritual bankruptcy,* whereby all the intellectual, physical, and financial resources I could garner still failed to achieve the results I was looking for. I could never get enough of what I truly didn't need. Some become willing when they see the **light**, others not until they feel the **heat.** I had to feel the heat—a profound sense of impending doom, emptiness, and feeling lost. This left me in a position of being open to seek a *spiritual solution* to this *spiritual problem.*

I use these words to describe what happened with the perspective I have today. But back in 1988 when this process began, I had no idea what was happening to me or within me. I somehow received the **Gift Of Desperation**, which led me to reach out for help. Because my addiction buddy and the only friend I had left on the planet got into recovery, and because I had run out of ideas, I became open to doing the same. I joined a *spiritual community*, a tribe of wounded healers comprised of countless circles of people committed to seeking a spiritual way of life.

When I was new to this community, I felt very uneasy, sort of like the proverbial long-tailed cat in a room full of rocking chairs. I thought I was seeking help in order to save my butt, not my soul; it was awhile before I realized they were connected. It took a lot of trial and error, attempting to remain self-reliant and invulnerable, and enduring gobs of emotional pain while physically recovering to conclude that although the monkey was off my back, the circus still hadn't left town. I intuitively sensed that my unwillingness to trust was going to kill me.

My next surrender was to allow myself to be led to a *spiritual teacher.* Because he embodied qualities that I aspired to cultivate in myself— mainly a peaceful heart and a sense of usefulness to others—I became willing to do what he did in order to get what he got. John began helping me see that the mind makes a wonderful servant, but a terrible master. I had been living under the tyranny of a fear-based mind/ego. I sought liberation.

John began to share with me the *spiritual principles* that he had been taught by his teacher years before. First I learned what they were and how they related to each of the Twelve Steps and to each other. Then he showed me how to practice them in my everyday life. Over years of practice, and sharing them with others, these principles were internalized into my very being.

Staying true to this path, this community, this teacher, and these principles resulted in a psychic change or spiritual awakening, sufficient to recover from a hopeless state of mind and body (i.e., an allergy of the body coupled with an obsession of the mind) and maintain long-term, contented, useful recovery. An allergy is simply an abnormal reaction. My abnormal reaction is that upon first ingesting an addictive substance, a compulsion to take more is triggered.

An obsession is a thought that persists and overpowers all other thoughts, and that thought is to ingest the substance no matter what, to disregard any thought to the contrary. Succumbing to the thought leads to taking the action that triggers the allergy, and the disease takes over.

Only when the spiritual malady is overcome do we then straighten out mentally and physically. I am certain that if I do not continue to enlarge my spiritual life and treat my underlying spiritual malady, I am subject to a return to self-destructive thoughts and actions.

Why do I continue to participate in this spiritual community?

- To **co-create** a twelve-step meeting so that those who are still suffering know where to find those of us who are in recovery.

- To **behaviorally** demonstrate **acceptance** of my spiritual malady.

- To **connect** with old friends and make new friends.

- To **be reminded of the problem** and what happens if it is not treated on an ongoing basis.

- To **be reminded of the solution** and how to apply it to the problem for desirable results.

- To plug in to the **power of the fellowship of the spirit**, which exceeds the power of the disease.

- To rejoice in the shared **language of the heart**.

- To be in position to **pass it on.**

Just for today I live with a deep gratitude as a fortunate survivor of a progressive and deadly disease.

A clique vs. a community vs. a cult
By Steve

I have been aware of a few individuals declining to seek the help they need from twelve-step programs because of the mistaken impression that they are cliques, or worse yet, cults. Rather, they comprise a community, which is a unified body of individuals who share common interests. The following chart is my understanding of the characteristics that distinguish community from a clique or cult.

It is important to keep in mind that the first twelve-step meeting we attend may or may not be a good fit for us, just as in the case of the first restaurant or church we try. It may take some time, effort, and exploring to find our "tribe." It did for me. I also discovered that if I kept going to a meeting to see only what I could get, I eventually would come away feeling empty. It was when I began attending meetings with an intention of seeing what I could add to the meeting that I truly started to feel like I belonged. It was then that I realized I was no longer simply attending a meeting; I was participating in my group. One evident milestone of recovery is being transformed from a taker to a giver.

A Clique	A Community	A Cult
A narrow, exclusive circle or group	A unified body sharing common interests or purpose—often inclusive	A group of persons united by devotion or allegiance to a person, dogma, or religious veneration
Physically limited in size	Virtually unlimited potential: the recovery community has millions of members in hundreds of thousands of groups worldwide	Can employ physical captivity, isolation, deprivation, and threats of future physical harm
Status quo protected Low level of consciousness	Usually about learning Expanding consciousness	May use covert propaganda, indoctrination, and mind control
Focus can be about keeping others out	Focus is about the thriving of the community and its members	Strong focus on preventing defection at individual's expense
Power held in a few hands Social manipulation	Power often shared Rotation of leadership	Leader holds all power Authority has no accountability
Outsiders have no value	Newcomers welcomed	Outsiders perceived as threat
Narrow-minded focus	Open-minded focus	Fanatical focus to exclusion of rationality
Self-serving	Serving cause bigger than itself	Self-serving leader
Efforts may benefit very few	Efforts intended to benefit greater number	Efforts may benefit very few and harm many
Predominately immature energy	More mature energy present	Rigid containment of energy that is incongruent with cult's agenda
Typically transient, unsustainable	Potential for great sustainability, longevity, and positive legacy	Typically transient, unsustainable, leaving negative legacy
Typically having narrow-minded and trivial agenda	Wider-reaching, overt agenda	Characterized by intense, often covert agenda
Pseudo-intimacy at best	Potential for true intimacy	Can prey on dependency needs
Can produce petty wounds	Can promote healing	Can produce deep psychic wounds
Can be mean-spirited	Generosity of spirit can prevail	Unlimited evil potential

I've heard people say that such and such twelve-step fellowship didn't work for them, so they stopped going and failed in their recovery attempts. My experience is that twelve-step fellowships do not work for me, I work for them. I work for it (recovery), and it works if I work it. I had to work at feeding my addiction, so why wouldn't I have to work for my recovery? I was in fact willing to go to any length to feed my addiction and pay tremendous costs. I was told that if I put half or even a quarter of the energy I had put into feeding my addiction into my recovery efforts, I would be in good shape indeed.

Angie adds:

Along the lines of community, working together, and helping others, here is a wonderful piece on what we can learn from geese.

Lessons from Geese*

FACT 1

As each goose flaps its wings it creates an "uplift" for the birds that follow. By flying in a "V" formation, the whole flock adds 71 percent greater flying range than if each bird flew alone.

Lesson
People who share a common direction and sense of community can get where they are going quicker and easier because they are traveling on the thrust of one another.

FACT 2

When a goose falls out of formation, it suddenly feels the drag and resistance of flying alone. It quickly moves back into formation to take advantage of the lifting power of the bird immediately in front of it.

*Used by permission of Robert McNeish

Lesson
If we have as much sense as a goose, we stay in formation with those headed where we want to go. We are willing to accept their help and give our help to others.

FACT 3
When the lead goose tires, it rotates back into the formation and another goose flies to the point position.

Lesson
It pays to take turns doing the hard tasks and sharing leadership. As with geese, people are interdependent on each other's skills, capabilities and unique arrangements of gifts, talents, or resources.

FACT 4
The geese flying in formation honk to encourage those up front to keep up their speed.

Lesson
We need to make sure our honking is encouraging. In groups where there is encouragement, the production is much greater. The power of encouragement is the quality of honking we seek.

FACT 5
When a goose gets sick, wounded, or shot down, two geese drop out of formation and follow it down to help and protect it. They stay with it until it dies or is able to fly again. Then, they launch out with another formation or catch up with the flock.

Lesson
If we have as much sense as geese, we will stand by each other in difficult times as well as when we are strong.

2

WORKING OUR OWN PROGRAM

{ *It starts with trust. . .*

By Steve }

T rust vs. mistrust is a basic stage of human development. We either develop a sense that there are people and things in the world we can trust, or there is no one and nothing we can trust or rely upon. I hit adulthood as a card-carrying member of the latter camp. At an early age, I began to distrust my feelings and perceptions.

The Trust Parade

First I began to misguidedly feel that I could only trust **my own mind,** and that relief from life's difficulties could be found in activities and substances upon which I would later grow dependent.

Second, I began to trust **the promise of my active addiction**; it had an endless supply of misery to serve up if I simply held out my plate. In a moment of clarity I trusted that the sense of impending doom I was feeling was because doom was impending, if I didn't make changes.

Upon surrendering to the recovery fellowship and seeing the twelve-step group meet every week in the same location, with the same old-timers in their same seats, sharing experience after experience of the solution being successfully applied to the addiction problem, I began to trust the **group**.

Next I started to trust that these Twelve Steps being worked, these **spiritual principles** being practiced by members of the group, actually were working to keep them free from relapse. It worked if they worked it.

After nearly disastrous consequences (during my sickness before recovery and then my sickness in recovery), I stood before the grim reality that I was not long for this world if I didn't overcome my fear, false pride, and defiance, and work all Twelve Steps. But to do this I needed a step guide or sponsor. But the dilemma was—I didn't trust a single human being on the planet. I didn't even trust myself to know whom to trust. This left me to take a leap of faith. Could there be a higher perspective that could help me if I swallowed some false pride and got out of the way? I took a risk and trusted the loving life force I didn't understand to guide me to the right man. This higher power delivered big, and would continue to deliver. Slowly I began to trust **in another man** as I observed and experienced his commitment to living these recovery principles.

As I progressed in my step work, I did an inventory, uncovered and discovered my grosser handicaps and the harm I had done to others, and then made amends. I began to replace reliance on my self-will (which was being driven by my defects of character) with reliance on a power other than myself. Only then did I begin to see my **recovering self** as more trustworthy than my addicted self.

As I practiced these principles and experienced positive results, my trust in the **recovery process** deepened. Ultimately, I came to trust that these recovery principles, this recovery fellowship was the manifestation of a **loving life force** that I could access and benefit from, even if I didn't understand it.

Now all that remained was to be able to trust a woman. Looking back, I realize that I was beginning to trust Angie in a way I had never trusted another woman. For me, being able to trust Angie was key if I was to become willing to commit to spend my life with her.

Relying on a higher power, insecurity vs. faith
By Angie

I can recall various periods of extreme insecurity. For example, when we were dating and Steve broke a date or wanted a few days to himself, I thought he was going to break up with me. A friend's assurance that this was not true did not help. What did help was remembering that I was all right before we got together, and I could survive again without him. Turns out that the many years I spent single were helpful, after all.

I wasn't always sure that things were going to work out with Steve. After all, they had never worked out for me before in other relationships. I worried that he would leave me, not for another woman, but to go "hug trees," as I would somewhat jokingly put it. In the beginning of our marriage, I stayed conscious of how we would separate things if we split up, "just in case." It was probably more than five years before we started putting our photos in the same album. This was after one of us asked the other, "We are going to stay together, right? Then why have separate albums?"

Occasionally I would be having an insecure day and I would ask Steve, "Do you love me today?" He told me that I could just assume he did, and that if anything changed he would let me know. He writes me wonderful cards, all of which I save. Once I was looking for reassurance, and he wasn't in a very good place, so he suggested that I go read my cards. Actually, it did help!

Today I don't feel the insecurities that Steve will leave me or stop loving me. I feel settled and secure in our love and lifetime commitment. However, I am painfully aware, if I think about it, that anything could happen to anyone. People die around me. People I love have suffered horrendous health challenges. I cannot imagine my life without the fullness that Steve brings to it. I feel vulnerable. Really vulnerable. I think I feel even more vulnerable as time goes by. Sometimes dealing with grief and loss slips momentarily into anticipatory grief: what if something happens to Steve? I don't go there. I pray to God to help me deal with what is in front of me and to be of service.

So here I am, full circle, back to relying on God, and His name is not Steve. My faith insists that if I take appropriate actions, God will give me the strength to handle whatever challenges life presents. In the meantime, I take care of what is in front of me—first things first, one thing at a time. I love my husband dearly, but if I make him my higher power, my spiritual condition will suffer and I will not be able to be the best possible partner.

Sponsorship and passing it on
By Steve

A vital leg of my journey was deep ego deflation that made me teachable and capable of first taking direction from, then partnering with, a sponsor. Then imagine my surprise when one day I realized, *I have become the man I used to go looking for.* I no longer needed others to "save me" from myself and the disease. I continue to need others in order to pass it on, to share what was passed on to me—to keep the channel of grace open, flowing, and vibrantly alive.

What motivates me to pass it on? Why do I sponsor? My hope is that I carry a message of depth and weight. If I don't, I may easily get bored, feel useless, and leave my recovery program, as I have witnessed dozens of people do, with undesirable, even fatal results. This is what is meant by, "We must give it away in order to keep it." Sponsoring is a privilege and an adventure. There is no greater satisfaction in the world than witnessing the progress of new members, seeing the light emerge from their eyes. No substance or addictive activity in the world ever gave me this thrill.

It seems now that for me a significant amount of working the program is working with others. The psychic change, the change in attitude and outlook toward life that I experience by working with others is something that I was never able to achieve by working on myself. Self could not overcome self. It turns out that sponsoring is a key that unlocks me from the bondage of self, the excessive self-concern that ends up being self-defeating. Whether as sponsor or sponsee, sponsorship is a primary way my shortcomings have been addressed; it has offered a pathway to emotional maturity, requiring putting into practice the adage of "principles before personalities." It is simply another way I turn my life and will over to the care of a power greater than myself.

If this loving life force lives deep down within me and deep down within you, then the closer I am to you, the more immersed I am in this loving life force. I am no longer in isolation. It has been through mentoring relationships that I have learned to be intimate with others via the language of the heart.

I believe that for each of us in recovery there is at least one person we are destined to help through sharing our unique experience. I know of no greater esteemable act than helping a fellow human being who is suffering. If someone asks for my help, I trust it is no mistake, so I don't say no. It makes me shudder to consider this: what if the man I asked for help had said no? I believe that if a higher power puts someone in my life, I can't hurt him if I am committed to practicing the principles of the steps. There are some who believe that we haven't worked the Twelve Steps in their entirety until we have taken another through the Twelve Steps. If you say, "I'm not good at it," fine—find someone who is looking for a lousy sponsor.

The sponsor/sponsee relationship is as indefinable as a marriage. I've heard it explained that when some call sponsees "babies," it is not a derogatory connotation because babies are universally loved and are our hope for the future; they are vulnerable, unknowing, and needy like newcomers. When I was a newcomer, I was what could be called "slippery and hard to diaper." It took several years until I graduated to spiritual kindergarten.

As a sponsor, I don't show up because I'm a good guy, but because this is just what I do. It's what I was not only taught, but shown to do. I never want to forget that when I was asked, "Are you willing to go to any length for victory over addiction?" my reply was, "Yes!"

Finally, I was taught that men sponsor men. I don't hide out from my own gender; I get to rediscover my gender.

Dr. Bob Smith described his reasons to sponsor another alcoholic:

• Sense of duty

• It is a pleasure

• I'm paying debt to the man who took time to pass it on to me

• Insurance against possible slips

What I get from helping others
By Angie

People I sponsor do not realize how much they are helping me. When I sponsor, I am/or feel

• Honored by others' confidences

• Trusted, because I am trustworthy

• Useful

• Focused outside of myself, my own self-absorption

• Aware of my own growth through listening to someone who is where I used to be

• Grateful for my own recovery

• Reminded of the devastation of addiction

• Valued because my experience, although painful at the time, can help others

• Humble, as if it is not me but a greater power working

• Surprised by the wisdom I share that does not seem to come from my normal consciousness—often it is even what I myself needed to hear

• Amazed by the ideas that come to me

• Guided

Someone once asked me for help with her negative thinking. I asked her to write down her negative thoughts for a week. We then turned them into positive self-talk, using opposite language or solutions, keeping the statements in the present tense, and avoiding the use of negatives, such as, " I am *not* going to _____," or I do *not* have _____." In addition, the positive statement had to be something she could reasonably believe. For example, at one time I could not have taken in an affirmation of "I am beautiful." My head would immediately negate the statement by telling me that I was fat (which somehow erases any beauty in my world of negative thinking). However, I could believe, "I was born beautiful." (So, if the mind or "disease" immediately cancels the positive statement, the person should select a different statement.)

This was such a great exercise that I have used it with several people. The following chart gives some examples.

Negative Self-Talk	Positive Self-Talk
General low self-esteem and/or remorse	
I am a screw-up; I am a loser.	I am worthy of having my ultimate good.
I don't deserve another chance.	I am perfectly human and humanly perfect.
I failed, did not keep a commitment/ resolution to self.	I experience continuous growth.
I'm not enough; I don't _____ well enough.	I am enough; I have enough; and I do enough.
I won't be able to sponsor anyone because I have nothing to give.	I am gloriously co-creating with a loving higher power the life my creator intended.
	I can get back on the horse and move on.
	I live in the solution now.
	I can succeed.
	God loves and forgives me just as I would love and forgive a child, so I forgive myself too.
	Opportunities are abundant.
	I am beginning to see where my experience can benefit others; I have a lot to offer; I am ready to be of service.
Fear/worry/anxiety	
What if I or my loved ones get sick or die, I lose my income source, can't pay the rent, lose the house, can't find a place to live?	God is taking care of me even when I am not aware of it.
What if God forgot about me?	I live free from fear and obsession.
	I do the footwork and leave the results up to God.
	It keeps getting easier and easier to rely on my higher power.
	I experience greater and greater spiritual contact and contentment.
	I am more and more able to be where my feet are right now.
	I live in constant gratitude for every little thing.
	God is directing my attention to what He would have me do.
	I am safe right now.

continued on page 142

Negative Self-Talk	Positive Self-Talk
Financial/income/career	
I don't have enough money and/or I'll never earn enough money. I'm not a good provider. I'm bored, in a rut, hate my job, and am too old to get another. I'll be a bag lady someday.	There is plenty for everyone, including me. Abundance flows into my life exactly where it is needed. I prosper everywhere I turn. My soul is whole and adventurous. I am doing my true work with my true people. I thank God for the courage to ask for what I want and need. I am strong enough to embrace change. I am constantly learning and growing. I am getting more and more excited about life each day; I am finding much to interest me. I now create a wonderful new job.
Lovability/attractiveness	
I am not lovable. If people really knew me they wouldn't like me/no one could really love me/ there will never be anyone for me. My partner or spouse will leave me one day. I'll always be lonely. I am ugly/not attractive to men/afraid of men/ too old. I'll never lose weight. If only I were thin, then I would be happy/popular/married/ in a relationship, etc.	I am seeing more clearly how my disease lies to me. I keep growing more skillful at shifting to positive thoughts. I am lovable every moment of every day. I am nurtured mentally, physically, and spiritually. God is showing me I can be of service to others and give out love. I experience love wherever I go. People really love me for me. I joyfully attract loving, uplifting, and stimulating people into my experience. Infinite Intelligence is attracting to me a man with whom I am in perfect harmony. People are attracted to my radiant beauty and ideas. I am attractive inside and out. I deeply and completely love and accept myself. I am perfect, just as I am. I appreciate my body, it works hard and it works well, it takes me everywhere and allows me to enjoy life. I am living in my ideal body. I enrich the lives of my loved ones.

continued on page 143

Negative Self-Talk	Positive Self-Talk
Health/depression	
My body is broken and it cannot be fixed. I'm always going to be depressed. I am not getting any better. My body is deteriorating as I age. I won't be able to keep my recovery. I'll never get unstuck.	It is safe for me to heal; it is possible for me to heal; it is benefiting me to heal. I am grateful for every single thing I am able to do right now. I am ready to be healed. My healing is already in progress. Every day in every way I am getting better and better. God is healing my body and my mind now. Positive change keeps unfolding within me and around me. Life supports me in wonderfully surprising ways. I embrace and share my growing wisdom. Thy will, not mine be done.
Feeling overwhelmed/despair	
I can't do all of this; I am overwhelmed; I don't know what to do. How can I get ever through this? I'll never be able to solve this problem or get this done, and/or it won't be good enough. I have to _____.	First things first, one thing at a time. The journey of a thousand miles begins with the first step. I am fully capable of taking the next indicated step. I trust You, God. I am perfectly equipped to handle life's challenges, even when I have doubts. God gives me the strength to handle anything. God is in charge. This too shall pass. When God made time, He made enough of it. My load is light. My priorities are in perfect order. God is guiding me every day and in every way. I release to God easily. I am flexible and flowing. Everything is truly fine in the end; if it doesn't feel fine it must not be the end. I get to _____.

How does this demonstrate a benefit of sponsorship? I thought it was such a great exercise that I eventually tried tracking my own negative thoughts, with enlightening results. I would not have thought of doing that if I was not trying to help others. I also use a sponsor's guidance to help me to work effectively with others. One of my sponsors commented that much of our negative self-talk improves as we get further along in recovery, and I have found this to be true.

When I feel really overwhelmed, my favorite mantra is, "first things first, one thing at a time." I get to remember to take my own advice and to pray for help when I am feeling stressed. Just recently, I felt too busy to even go to a meeting, which was exactly what I needed to do. I went anyway, and after the meeting, I felt better. Somehow things did not seem so urgent or intense. I need to go to meetings and work with others to keep in fit spiritual condition, avoid taking unimportant things too seriously, and to be of service. My life is then much more enjoyable for both me and my loved ones, and even if I am tired, I receive energy to my spirit. Funny how that works.

EXERCISE

Pay attention to and make a list of your own negative thoughts. Review the list and add to it every day for a week. Then transform the thoughts into opposite, positive statements, using the present tense. Repeat these as affirmations during challenging times.

3

HONESTY/AUTHENTICITY

{ *"Fake it till you make it"* or
"to thine own self be true"? }

By Steve

Five Rules of "Civilized Society"*

1. You cannot have anything wrong with you.

2. If you do have anything wrong with you, get over it fast.

3. If you can't get over it fast, pretend that you did.

4. If you can't pretend, then drop out.

5. If you won't drop out, at least have the decency to look ashamed when you are around the rest of us.

*Derived from talks given by Father Tom W and originated by Father Terry R

Pretending

I didn't like my third-grade teacher. The first time I pretended to be sick, my Nana was summoned to watch over me while my parents were away. I was allowed to spend the day propped up by a mountain of pillows in my parents' big bed because their bedroom held the household's only working television.

I watched *Bonanza* (while eating the cinnamon toast Nana delivered on a tray) and *Mayberry RFD* while sipping tomato soup in between bites of a tuna sandwich. I was delighted to discover that our home's "no soda" rule was waived on sick days, so I got to drink two whole bottles of 7UP. I had hit the jackpot, and ended up missing twenty-six days of school that year.

By the time I began recovery in 1988 at age thirty-one, I was truly sick. I was so sick, in fact, that I thought I was well, other than some out-of-control substance abuse. I believed that if I could just get a handle on my addiction, the rest of my life would magically fall into place. I was totally blind to the pervasive defects of character that interfered with my ability to keep a job, be in a relationship, or follow through on my perpetually postponed dreams of travel, education, and financial security.

After being in recovery a few years but still struggling, in desperation I sought out a guy named John P, who, rumor had it, was a straight-shooter and had helped a lot of people. I had been suffering anxiety attacks for many years, and one day John asked me if I knew what caused them. "I wish I did," I replied, "do you?" I reacted strongly at first, and judged his explanation to be flip, over-simplified, and downright cruel. He told me that anxiety was caused by pretending—pretending to be someone I wasn't. After a few days of sulking, I began to hear a ring of truth in his words. Instead of being well and pretending to be sick as I did in the third grade, now I was sick and pretending to be well.

Wanting to look good and be liked, I kept trying to share in meetings about how much I knew and how well I was doing, while I was dying inside. One day I heard someone say that I couldn't save my face and my ass at the same time. John assured me that if I could get real, find out who I was, and simply be that person, I'd find peace. Eventually I did, and eventually I did.

A Funny Thing Happened on the Way to Authenticity. . .

"Fake it till you make it," I would hear. This seemed to be in direct contradiction with "To thine own self be true." It turned out that becoming willing to take "contrary action"— show up to a meeting, be of service, and tell the truth, even (especially) when I didn't feel like it, was afraid, or tired—was a lifesaver. Today I'll take inauthentic courage over authentic fear any day. This approach has also translated into being a better partner to Angie. Sometimes compromising doesn't feel like being true to myself until I remember that I am being true to my love for Angie and true to my commitment to what is best for our union.

What's So Difficult about Being Honest?

Starting out on this journey of recovery, the only thing I knew about honesty was how to spell it. I had so much practice living dishonestly that I became a mystery even to myself.

One definition of D.E.N.I.A.L.: Don't Even Notice I Am Lying… to myself!

Somewhere along the line I learned the coward's bargain: I won't call you on your stuff if you don't call me on mine. After all, living in truth can be messy, inconvenient, and uncomfortable. But can living a lie ever offer us more? My ego has experienced spiritual progress as one insult after another.

I am grateful for elders who help me see the subtlety of my dishonesty and the damage it causes. I am grateful to every single man and woman who exhibits the courage to share honestly in a twelve-step meeting. For it is clear that honesty is an essential ingredient to a healthy soul.

The Challenge of Staying Awake in Relationship

All behavior falls into one of two categories: extending love or asking for love. Sometimes we can ask for love so unskillfully that it can be mistaken for something else. I believe relationships die a thousand slow deaths through words spoken, decisions made, and actions taken from a place of unconsciousness vs. truly being awake to what is going on around us and what is going on *within us.*

I know I carried distorted beliefs about what it meant to be a man and a husband. I also carried some twisted ideas about women and what a wife was supposed be and do. For many years I held an image of the marriage I didn't want, but had no conscious awareness and no vision of the partnership I yearned for. I often acted on unconscious expectations, and reacted to mates who didn't meet needs I didn't even know I had and certainly couldn't put into words. I did not have the ability to hear the meta-message or the true message beneath the surface message. What was my partner really saying? What was I really saying to my partner? What was I really saying to myself as I justified my unskillful behavior?

So often an emotional overreaction clouded out reason, or an over-reliance on intellect kept me disconnected from my heart. It was a revelation when I could finally see that so much of my anger sprang from the fact that I couldn't feel love. My heart was so guarded, mistrusting, and inaccessible. Over the years, the language of the heart, extended through thousands of shares heard at meetings, has helped soften and open my heart.

Are We Ever Too Broke to Pay Attention?

Pay attention to your thoughts for they become your words...

Pay attention to your words for they become your actions...

Pay attention to your actions for they become your habits...

Pay attention to your habits for they will shape your character...

Pay attention to your character for it shall shape your destiny!*

*author unknown

On being real

By Angie

Why am I afraid to express my true feelings?

• I don't want to rock the boat.

• I want to avoid conflict.

• You might stop loving me.

• You might judge or criticize, say I am wrong for feeling the way that I do.

• You might even use my statements against me later.

• Self-judgment (e.g., if I were working a better program or if I were a better person, I would not even feel this way, especially about things that I am judging as trivial).

So, when I tell you my truth I may feel extremely vulnerable, raw, or exposed. I am risking your rejection and may fear that I am giving you my power. I need to really trust you. And you need to treat my feelings in a respectful, trustworthy way.

I once made the mistake of asking Steve if he missed me when he had been away for a day. He responded, "Not yet, sometimes it takes two or three days." Would it have killed him to just say "yes"? The flip side of this is that I trust every word he says. When he tells me, "I miss you already" the first day of my absence, I believe him. Being authentic with each other means that

• I don't always hear what I want (did I want him to lie?).

• I don't ask questions that I might not like the answers to (e.g., the old "does my butt look fat in these pants?").

• I need to honor him and his feelings, treating his disclosure as if it is a sacred trust.

I've heard it said that the good news about recovery is that you feel better; the bad news is that you feel everything better. The message here is that when we are not distracted by our addiction, we are free to deal with reality—life on life's terms, as they say. It makes me crazy when I hear people discounting feelings. I heard someone in a meeting say he was having negative feelings going through a divorce, and therefore, he wasn't working a good program. What I don't understand is why we think we shouldn't have the same feelings experienced by the rest of the population, just because we were addicted to substances or compulsive behavior and are now in recovery.

In my experience, it was when I was running to escape my feelings that I was really in trouble. That is what drove a host of compulsive/addictive behaviors. When I simply allow myself to feel, without turning to a substance or destructive escape behavior, the feelings pass. I am allowing the feelings, not causing them. There is a big difference. In addition, I am usually not engaging in behaviors that cause even more problems. I've heard it said that "recovery is like the springs on a bad mattress: when you push one down, another pops up." In other words, people may enter recovery from substance addiction, only to succumb to one or more of other kinds of addictive behavior, such as compulsive gambling, shopping, or overeating; sex and love addiction; or extreme codependency. For me, denial can be dangerous. After all, before recovery, didn't we spend our whole lives trying to escape from feelings, whether through alcohol, drugs, food, inappropriate relationships, shopping, or getting addicted to other peoples' drama? I now have a higher power and a program of recovery to help me, but I still need to admit/acknowledge the feelings, experience them, and move on as soon as I am able.

Grief vs. self-pity
By Steve

A few months into my recovery process, I had an experience I am never likely to forget. I came home from work and no one was home;

the house was quiet. I stepped through the front door, paused, and stood in the living room listening to the silence, feeling the stillness. All of a sudden I became aware of emptiness in my gut that pushed against my heart, causing me to exhale more deeply. Next thing I knew I was exhaling in short bursts, the air being pushed out of my lungs, and I collapsed sobbing onto the hardwood floor.

What the hell was going on? For an instant, I became aware that my mind wanted to figure this out, and come up with a reason for why I was crying. I am so thankful I set that aside and allowed myself to go with it. I trusted in that moment that more would be revealed later, but for right now, the greatest gift I could give myself was being present with what was here now—grief.

Before recovery, in the unlikely event that the conversation turned to talk of "grief," I would have to excuse myself, for grief was like a creature whose acquaintance I had avoided.

But now here it was in my living room, in my chest, sucking the breath out of me, pouring down my cheeks, causing me to curl up in a fetal position, and taking me into a blackness I had never experienced. Again my first impulse was to recoil, avoid, or at least postpone this strange experience from going any further. But my deeper instinct supported me in embracing this sorrow. Alongside this trusting, in this letting go, there was a compelling curiosity. Recovery had begun to feel like an adventure, and this was simply another new place to be explored.

What I later discovered, strongly connected to this grief, was awareness that I missed my gramps. Growing up, my gramps was like an anchor that kept me tethered to the mother ship.

My gramps died suddenly of a heart attack while painting the preacher's house when I was fourteen years old. You'll never guess what age I began using alcohol and other drugs to medicate grief too big to hold, too mysterious to process.

Seventeen years after Gramp's passing, one of the first things I noticed upon emerging from this grieving episode was that I could move my head more freely; the muscles in my neck were no longer tighter than piano wires. I felt like a couple of bowling balls had been lifted from my shoulders. I could take a deeper breath that felt cleansing. I felt a sense of calm and acceptance that was alien.

On occasion, in meetings when I tried to express grief, there were some members who were visibly uncomfortable and vocalized that dis-ease through admonitions that I "get off my pity pot." Because those assertions did not ring true to me, it awakened a curiosity in me to explore what distinguished grief from self-pity. Below is what I came up with.

Self-pity	Grief
A frustration arising from thwarted, self-centered grasping	A heartfelt response to a legitimate loss
Toxic, life-eroding	Tonic, life-enhancing
Full of self	Emptying of self
Coming from the mind	Coming from the heart
Tears = monument to "my suffering is unique" (set self apart from humanity)	Tears = true healing, connecting to commonalty of legitimate human suffering. Shared grief can be a basis for community, true intimacy
Never-ending cloud cover	No rain, no rainbows
Pity party deadens spirit	Grieving opens door to spirit
Leads to more focus on self	Results in expanded compassion for, service to others
Evidence of disconnection from true self and inner-guidance system	Path to greater connectedness to true self and inner-guidance system
Never letting up	Letting go
Resolution impossible, stay stuck Endless dead-ending cycle	Dissolving barriers, open up expressive pathway Leads to inner peace, emotional freedom
A heavy mood, bogs us down	A wave that washes over and moves on, leaving us light

continued on page 153

Self-pity	Grief
It's about "not enough" (me, you, life is never enough)	It's about abundance, an overflowing heart (someone or something of great value has been lost)
I'm building a case that I'm unlovable	I love and am loved; I feel loss of beloved; I can grieve because I have loved
Symptom of heart closed, hardening	Evidence of heart opening, softening
Shadow, self-dishonesty Trying to convince self reality should be different	Emotional honesty: accepting transitory sadness, reality of loss, reality as it is
Poor me, poor me, pour me a drink Would you like some cheese with your whine? Sniveling, difficult to listen to	Clear sharing regarding what had value, now gone Witnessing, being present more doable (if you've done your own grief work)
Staying on surface is less threatening but is a boring landscape that grows unfulfilling	Allowing oneself to sink deep into rich feeling world is strange/scary at first and requires courage

What support looks like to me

By Angie

When Steve and I had been dating only a few months, my dear mother was diagnosed terminally ill and died within one month. When I reflect on how Steve handled that, it still touches me very deeply. In his loving support, he

• Let me have my feelings—really honored them

• Never told me not to feel that way

• Never tried to get me to "snap out of it"

• Gave good hugs

• Asked me what I needed

It was also around that time he wrote the chart outlining the differing characteristics of grief and self-pity. For some reason, the very distinction between grief and self-pity was helpful and comforting to me. I have shared the chart with many people who have also found it useful. I feel sad that when people are in extreme pain, they sometimes beat themselves up for feeling that way. Like it isn't enough that we suffer, but then we have to suffer for suffering because we should be happy all the time!

Sometimes people talk about feeling sorry for themselves, or having a "pity party." My early recovery was characterized by self-pity. How did that look? One example is feeling sorry for myself because I did not have a boyfriend. Grief is much different; it is about losing something or someone of great value, like my mother, who is now gone. I found healing in allowing myself the permission to feel sad when that is the way I felt. Again, I'm not creating or holding onto grief, just allowing myself to experience it. By doing so, I find that I can be crying one minute and laughing the next. I also find that my capacity to be there for others in their grief has greatly expanded. One of my best coping mechanisms is to acknowledge the feelings and then get into service.

How can unacknowledged grief affect a relationship? I have experienced grief as a strange and shifting animal. We can have reactions that we may not even associate as being connected to the grief process. I need to stay conscious so that I don't blame my partner for my misery or snap at him, then justify my actions as being caused by something he said, did, or neglected.

When I am unaware of my grief, my mind can make up something to blame for my unhappiness. For example, in the late nineties I was surprised to be feeling sorry for myself because I did not have a boyfriend. I thought, "What is going on? I haven't felt this way in a long, long time." Then I remembered that my best friend had died a week earlier. I marveled that I had been feeling sad (grief) and that my brain had made up a reason why.

After my father died I was comparing notes with a friend whose father had passed away one week before. I discovered occurrences (like inability to concentrate, losing things, inertia, etc.) that I probably would not have otherwise attributed to the grief process, especially because they continued for a long time after the death. I might have been wondering what was wrong with me if my friend who had also lost her father was not having similar experiences. Grief can definitely affect a relationship, and it is sad that some marriages don't survive tragic losses such as the death of a child.

Recently, Steve and I had a discussion at our Valentine's couples retreat where we realized that we had both been handling recent losses in different ways. There are many things in life that can trigger grief. Steve had already been experiencing some sorrow, when a twenty-seven-year-old young man, who was like part of our family, died of an overdose. We were both grief-stricken and had been handling it in different ways. Mine was to get into activity, scheduling previously postponed work around the house in order to check these accomplishments off my list (maybe to "take charge" of something I could actually control in life). Steve's preference was to have more quiet, solitude, and reflective time. Obviously, our methods were in conflict, especially when Steve woke up to painters in the master bathroom. So grief, especially when unacknowledged, can put a strain on a relationship, and may cause us to have conflicts about trivial things that aren't really the problem.

There are times when I may need to seek support outside of my primary relationship. One of my mentors made the observation that relationships tend to break up when both people become crazy at the same time. They each perceive the other as not being supportive. This is one reason that it is not a good idea to expect any one person to meet all of our needs. It is helpful to cultivate friendships outside of the marriage, and to know when we need to rely more heavily on them, or on other family, mentors, church groups, and maybe even professionals.

When my mother died, I went to a grief support group, primarily for the benefit of my daughter. I didn't think I needed it myself because

I was talking about my feelings in other groups. However, the grief group was very different. I don't know what is helpful about crying your guts out with other people who are in the same kind of pain, but I do know that it helped. The rest of society doesn't seem to have a place for deep loss beyond the initial shock and funeral services. Sometimes the pain far outlasts the tolerance and support of friends and family, and it comes in waves.

The hero's journey of recovery

By Steve

Recently, in working with a man I sponsor who had begun touching some grief, I reflected on my own encounters with grief. I sat down to shoot off a quick email to him, summarizing a few points I thought might be helpful. Next thing I knew a few points turned to forty, and I had relived that last twenty-two years of recovery, including a pivotal period of my life when I was introduced to the idea of the hero's journey. It occurred to me that there was a parallel between recovery and a hero's journey. There are three parts to a hero's journey:

1. Preparation and the call

2. The journey of answering the call

3. The return

Whereas one's story of recovery can be told as

1. What it was like

2. What happened

3. What it's like now

What Is a Hero's Journey?

The sacred passage of a person's life could be described as a hero's journey that begins with a descent so painful (ego deflation at depth) that one is compelled to leave one's current lifestyle/living situation and go on a journey to seek and discover a better way to live. The journey provides challenges to overcome, supportive allies and obstructive foes, and possibly even dragons to slay along the way. A dragon can be seen as a metaphor, symbol, or archetype of an obstacle, whether it is external or internal.

An **archetype** can refer to anything from a universally understood symbol to a characterization of a complex constellation of behaviors and ways of being. Examples of some archetypes are Innocent, Orphan, Caregiver, and Sage. Addiction employs the archetypal energies of the Destroyer, the misguided Seeker, and non-evolved Fool. Four major guiding archetypes of the human mind are Lover, Warrior, Magician, and King/Queen.

Discovering how and when to engage these contrasting energies (or aspects of being in the world) can lead to a more cohesive (vs. conflicted) self and inner peace (vs. restlessness, irritability, and discontentedness.) My hero's journey has both called upon these archetypal energies and helped them evolve, enabling me to be more skillful in my relationship with myself, others, and a power greater than myself. Just as addiction is progressive, so is recovery. The following is one way to describe my recovery or hero's journey up until this writing.

One Man's Understanding and Experience

- Waking up in recovery is awesome *and* can be accompanied by all kinds of feelings.

- I like looking good and feeling good and welcome the "good" feelings.

- I didn't like the "bad" feelings and consciously or unconsciously attempted to avoid them.

- I never found a way to only feel good *and* still keep the expressive pathway (heart) open and flowing.

- I am capable of confusing what is "good" for me and what is "bad" for me. Just look at my history.

- Waking up involved waking up to how asleep I was and the price I pay for sleepwalking.

- Waking up also involved the price other people have paid for my sleepwalking. (These feelings were especially unpleasant.)

- In waking up I felt a sense of loss for lost years being asleep. Loss triggers grief. Grief brings tears.

- I once believed tears made me look bad and weak. Now I deeply respect men who can cry.

- I don't trust men who can't cry. I hold compassion for them, and I hold a space for their grief.

- I had no practice grieving and therefore was not skillful at it.

- I don't like doing or trying to do things I'm not quickly skillful at, thus I discovered yet another motive to avoid grieving.

- I either allow myself to grieve and also get to feel joy, passion, and vibrant life, or I don't—and I don't.

- Reality will not budge on this one. To avoid this truth, I must go into shadow (unenlightened self).

- There is a fat menu of options (ways to avoid grief). They all are destructive to me and others.

- I cannot run away from myself without saying "yes" to falling back to sleep and living in shadow.

- Feeling trapped makes me feel angry. I feel temporarily more powerful in anger than grief.

- Anger is not good or bad, it's like fire—it all depends on how it's used.

- Anger is a gateway emotion to the Warrior. My warrior is poised to fight my inner obstacles to awakening, but can sometimes misguidedly focus on shortcomings of others.

- Unexpressed feelings remain waiting to be expressed and will come out sideways in hurtful digs.

- A great blessing is finding safe people and safe places where my grief/anger is welcome.

- People who are running from their own grief/anger will not be comfortable around mine.

- Grief is the gateway emotion to the Lover. I discovered that my anger was about not being able to feel love.

- Fear is the failure of self-reliance. Fear is the gateway emotion to the Magician…the Great Magician (i.e., God)!

- He who fears he will suffer already suffers what he fears. I can starve fear with faith.

- Courage is not the absence of fear, but being willing to act despite the fear in order to take healthy risks.

- When I allow myself to be real and my heart to open, I feel joy. Joy is the gateway emotion to the King (higher self).

- Joy shared is doubled; grief shared is halved. Honest feelings shared are one basis for unity in humanity.

continued on page 160

- In awakening to my human beingness, I see that life involves legitimate suffering and that my suffering is not unique.

- I am a spiritual being having a human experience—ten-thousand joys and ten-thousand sorrows, a package deal.

- All of life supports my spiritual path. My ego experiences spiritual progress as one insult after another. Get over it, I must remind myself.

- All of this is much too important to take too seriously; laughter is medicine for the soul.

- The journey of recovery for me is the transformation from self-centeredness to centered selfness.

- From centered selfness there's nothing left to do but enjoy living, loving, and sharing on this amazing planet.

- The honest sharing of feelings leads to healing. I have become the man I used to go looking for.

- In awakening to who I am, I embrace my past as being the price of knowledge and for its value to the future. I have come to see how my experience can benefit others. None of it was wasted.

- When my King is awake, my Lover, my Warrior, and my Magician are integrated and in balance, my life works.

- I need others to help me stay awake. I welcome people in my life to point out when I'm in shadow.

- I believe it is in my own enlightened self-interest to remember, practice, and share the above.

In concluding this portion on keeping the "I" in marriage, we emphasize that we must each honor our own spiritual path, as well as our partner's spiritual needs, while still being committed to our partnership. It is as whole individuals that we come together to form a single, loving unit.

PART V

"Passing It On"

as a Couple

1

THEY STOOD AT
THE TURNING POINT

{ *Inspiration from other couples* }

Ours is only one story. We were inspired by many people who overcame backgrounds similar to ours, yet achieved healthy relationships. We are including examples of how some other couples in recovery have weathered relationship storms. These stories offer varying perspectives, and we hope our readers will identify with something that encourages them that they, too, can survive substantial challenges.

Patrick and Candice

Patrick and Candice's marriage has survived for forty-four years,
despite the ravages of active addiction, as he recounts:

*My wife Candice and I were high school sweethearts. We married
at twenty-one and moved to Hawaii for our first years of marriage.
Life was good. We both refer to this time in our marriage as our
"ignorant bliss phase" mainly because we had no clue of how to be
married or how to "do" a relationship, but we both thought we were
deeply in love, without knowing the real meaning of the word.*

*After moving back home to California we sailed through ten years,
seemingly with no problems. We were pursuing the "American dream"
of a house, kids, a second car, and a credit card. To achieve this, we
determined that we needed two incomes. So, Candice went back to
work. She provided extremely well for the family and had a very
successful career. However, it took a toll on her. She became addicted
to alcohol, and it affected not only her but the entire family as well.
This began our "active addiction phase." I was extremely angry,
frustrated, confused, and hurt. I thought her addiction was a moral
issue. My feeling was that if she really loved me, she would quit. Many
times she promised to stop, only to relapse a few days later.*

*In the years that followed, our marriage deteriorated dramatically.
We were on a merry-go-round and couldn't get off. We were in
denial, with lots of fear and lack of faith. We had been married for
twenty-two years at the time when I made a decision to separate
from her and move out. I knew in my heart that I still loved this
woman, but I couldn't live like that anymore. I never believed that
we would call it quits, but here we were looking down the barrel of
a divorce. Candice would subsequently go through five treatment
centers in three-and-a-half years. I was ready to accept that she
could not recover. This was the lowest point in our marriage. I have
never felt more emotional pain than when we were apart. Both of us
reached our "bottoms." Fortunately, I found a twelve-step recovery
program that helped me realize that I had been affected by this*

disease and that it was time for me to take my eyes off of my wife and focus on me. This was the turning point for both of us.

After a gran mal *seizure that almost killed Candice, and a spiritual experience that followed, a miracle happened. In her words, she was "struck sober." About this time, I had what I call my spiritual awakening. I had gone one-on-one with addiction, and I lost. I raised the white flag and decided to surrender. I finally came to understand and believe in my heart that this was a disease and not a moral issue. I began to feel compassion for Candice and what she was going through.*

This was the beginning of our "recovery phase." We both became active in our respective recovery programs. This also included attending meetings for couples in recovery. We would both work our individual recovery programs, which gave us a good foundation. Then we would go to our weekly couples meeting and discover information that would help us to learn how to be married, how to build a meaningful relationship, how to communicate in a healthy way, and how to develop real intimacy and understand the meaning of unconditional love. With help from our sponsors and many friends in the fellowship, we were also encouraged to attend weekend couples retreats. We attend two retreats a year, and these have been extremely beneficial in our recovery as a couple. Our marriage is not perfect. It has its ups and downs, but we have tools that help us to get through the rough times and celebrate the good times. Today, more than half of our married years have been in recovery. We both understand that recovery is a journey, not a destination. We have learned to embrace whatever comes our way because we know that we have found a solution and a way of life that works.

Chuck and Debbie

Chuck and Debbie have been in recovery since February 18, 1983 and September 23, 1976, respectively. They had their first date on February 15, 1985, and have been married since July 13, 1985. Debbie writes:

Chuck and I met, and very soon afterward (a week later) I said, "This seems to be going pretty fast; what do you expect out of this?" His response was, "I want to collect Social Security with you." What a guy! Well that has come true as of this month, and we have been married more than twenty-five years.

Chuck and I met at a meeting. I sat in front of him and he rubbed my shoulders. You can't get any better than that. I needed an escort to a recovery banquet for a program that my kids were involved in, and I noticed that Chuck wore a suit to meetings. I figured that he must have a job and he had a car—a perfect escort. We were married five months later.

About six months after we were married, Chuck took a job that required him to leave home on Monday and return on Friday every week. This was perfect for two independent people who were suddenly living together. For the next fifteen years, his job required him to be away from home for long periods of time, and permitted him to come home on weekends. His last assignment was in Philadelphia, and we only saw each other every three weeks or so. The assignment was to be only for six months, but ended up lasting for two-and-a-half years. This was not a good thing for our marriage. Because he was away, he did not know the people I talked about, the ones I knew from meetings and the gals that I sponsored, and I didn't know the people he talked about from the meetings that he went to. We started to drift apart emotionally, spiritually, and physically; we were not together enough.

In the meantime I had set up my own business at home. We had an office built over the garage, and I was off with my business doing mortgage loans. I was so busy that I was working all the time— days, nights, and weekends. I was having a difficult time finding anyone who had the experience to be able to help me. When Chuck's assignment ended, there was not a position with his company anywhere in California. I made the suggestion that he come and work with me, since I was unable to keep up with the business that I had. Everyone we talked to thought we had lost our minds. So of course with that kind of support…the only thing to do was to go forward with our idea.

So there we were—me a banker for twenty-seven years and in the mortgage business for ten years, and Chuck who had been a CFO of hospitals for over thirty-five years—trying to set up a partnership that required me to teach him how to process mortgage loans. To make it more difficult, I am an extrovert who thinks with my mouth, and Chuck is an introvert who processes quietly. You can imagine the challenges we had. I was talking and talking to get my information across to Chuck, and he was not responding because he was trying desperately to process what I was telling him, while I was giving him even more information. I was in charge of teaching him everything I knew about the mortgage business. We were beginning to think this was a really dumb idea. But remember the office we built over the garage? Well, when the day ended we shut the door, walked down the stairs, walked into our home—and never took the work home with us.

Part of our business plan was to see our therapist once a week in the beginning to have her coach us on how to make this work. We also each had our separate twelve-step meetings, people we sponsored, friends, and family. We had our together time, and we continued to go to our couples group meetings and retreats. We supported each other's passions. Chuck is a bicyclist, and I love to teach freeform crochet. We also set up a movie date for every Friday night. We are still doing that today, more than ten years later.

The lessons we learned were many. We each function differently, and neither one is right or wrong. We each have the same goals and want to achieve those goals. We each walk a different path, but in the *same direction. Our God and our program come first, and if we keep that in perspective the rest of our lives, it will work just fine.*

God put two souls together who had many lessons to learn. Through learning these lessons, we each have become closer to our spiritual soul and have become better human beings. Our life is more than we deserve, and we are forever grateful for what we have been given and what lies ahead for us in our coming years of retirement.

John and Mary

Around 1994, when Mary had about twenty years of recovery in Al-Anon and John had been in recovery for thirteen years, they reached a crisis point in their marriage of seven years. Mary writes:

About seven years ago, my husband and I were on the verge of a divorce. I had purchased tickets to a religious retreat and made reservations at a local hotel where the retreat was being held. We stayed Friday and Saturday night. It was during the month of May, and the weather was very nice. The only reason my husband went (he said) was because I had paid the hotel room in advance and invited him to participate.

By Sunday morning, after a writing exercise in which we were instructed to write a letter to each other describing what first attracted us to the other person, my husband had written nothing, and I had written a list of things. We exchanged "letters." When I saw that he had written nothing, I was stunned. I immediately began making arrangements in my head about where I was going to live, how we would split up the furniture, and so forth. I was determined not to let this ruin my life. And I was through "trying."

By Sunday afternoon, my husband was asking me for forgiveness and asking me if I would be willing to start again to work on our relationship. Again I was stunned. I was preparing to leave, or have him leave and then live on my own, happily. I told him I could not make such a sharp U-turn in my emotions, and that I would think about it. I asked him what had happened during the sessions we had attended that made him change his mind. (The men had been in one session, while the women were in a separate session for about two hours). He replied that the leader of his session asked the men what they would say to God on judgment day, when He asked, "How did you treat my daughter?"

We worked out the immediate discord from that weekend; we each used our own twelve-step program to keep us honest with ourselves, our friends, family, and acquaintances, and especially with God. Our programs help us stay close to our higher power (whom we call God). Our relationship is not a "happily ever after" story. It takes work and prayer, meetings and reasoning things out with others. It's worth it to attempt to do God's will; the rewards are serenity, hope, and love.

Bob and Ginny

Bob and Ginny just celebrated forty-three years of marriage. They demonstrate that a relationship can survive serious challenges, even the loss of a child. Bob writes:

Ginny and I met forty-four years ago on the rebound from other marriages; she was twenty-three, and I was thirty-two. We married after the first year together. Her father was stern, an engineer, who ruled the home with an iron hand, which occasionally found its way to physically disciplining Ginny. But a day never passed that the bills were not paid. By contrast, I was a handsome, fun-loving guy. Both our educated families had teaching backgrounds, and we were both educated ourselves. I taught Ginny to drink, and we passed the first years enjoying each other before other things entered our lives.

Our journey began hedonistically and ended spiritually. For seventeen-and-a-half years we drank together, and it began as fun. As reality and children arrived, the fun-loving Bob proved a contrast to Ginny's father, that solid wage earner with disciplined spending, who created a wonderful estate. I, on the other hand, had an alcoholic father and learned from him to live hand-to-mouth, and as a result, we often redeemed soda bottles to buy our beer. The honeymoon was soon over; our natural love held the union together, but it was easy to see the differences in the way we had been raised. Ginny found that when you married, you got the whole package.

We had three children, and although we were loving parents, alcohol had begun to strongly influence our family. I went from job to job, and though I was wildly entrepreneurial, the businesses often failed. Ginny was rethinking her "fun" husband. Alcohol was directing my life; as I review those years I have come to believe that Ginny drank so she could tolerate my behavior. We were truly a very dysfunctional family, and sadly, our children were influenced by our behavior. I had three children by my former marriage, and my oldest son was injured in an accident influenced by my lifestyle, was badly brain-damaged, and died some years later. Two bankruptcies and a white-collar crime with a short prison sentence followed. Life was not sweet!

As my surviving son followed me into addiction, I was able to recognize his addiction without acknowledging my own. At age seventeen, he came home loaded one evening and a scene followed that made Ginny realize she could no longer live that way. She went to her bedroom and prayed for help; the next day she called Alcoholics Anonymous.

Ginny found a sensitive way to invite me to a meeting, and on January 6, 1986, we began a spiritual journey that has completely changed our lives. Ginny "got" the program immediately, and we discovered, by one of those spiritual "coincidences," a group called Couples in Recovery. Since that first meeting we have attended around 1250 meetings of that fellowship. We have never been the same.

Life did not become wonderful immediately; there was a lot to learn, and we learned at very different speeds. Ginny reverted to many of the lessons of her youth, and after a few years of recovery she concluded that I would never earn another penny, so she went back to college. She first earned a bachelor's degree in social work, and then her master's degree. She began a career as a child protective services worker, and with a steady income we began to recover financially. I had become a "mister mom," having to stay home and do the work that Ginny had done and no longer had the time for.

With my new integrity, I was able to begin to slowly become successful. Ginny had gone back to church and had God in her life, and I was challenged to do the same. I had to make the decision to believe, and to my amazement found a spiritual life of my own. We began attending church together, where I was elected an elder, and am now a respected deacon in a large church. We read various books each morning, and have a time of prayer that centers us for the day.

We learned that our program is one of attraction, and our new spiritual life together has attracted our children back to us and to recovery also. We have two children in the program now and another child who is a budding psychologist (he may be afraid to drink). We have a successful business, financial stability, and are enormously happy—all for turning our life and our will over to God as we understand him. We travel down the "road of happy destiny," a spiritual road.

Eric and Lucy

Lucy got into recovery in May of 1985, and married Eric six years later. Her story demonstrates how counseling and working a recovery program saved their marriage and family. She writes:

My husband was raised in an alcoholic home, and I am in recovery. We both believe in and practice the principles of recovery in our lives and our marriage. There was a time when I thought that marriage counseling was for people who had a bad relationship, and ours was happy and in need of no help. But after we had been married fourteen years, our marriage was in trouble. We both had high-level, demanding jobs, and we were raising two young children. The unresolved resentments that we had picked up in our marriage and the differences in our needs as individuals had driven a wedge between us.

My years in recovery had taught me that I needed to have the courage to change the things I could, and we sought professional help. We made a commitment to go to counseling every week no matter how hard it got—and believe me, there were times that we wanted to quit and to give up. But in recovery we learned that we had to face our fears, and if we wanted our marriage to survive, we had to do the work. In therapy we learned how to honor each other's needs without abandoning our own needs. We came to accept and embrace our differences, making compromises when necessary to honor the other's needs. Our honest communication helped us to understand that our individual needs and personality differences were not something we could change, but we could accept them in our partner and not take them personally. Today we know who we are, and we are in acceptance of who our partner is. I believe that seeking outside help is not a sign of a weak relationship, but rather an indication of courage and strength. I am grateful for the help that we received, and I am not sure where we would be today if we had not sought outside help. My husband and I have been married now for twenty years, and we are blessed with a wonderful marriage and friendship built on mutual respect and a deep and abiding love for which I am deeply grateful.

Chris and Jan

Chris and Jan's story demonstrates how persistence can sometimes save even a seemingly hopeless marriage. Jan writes:

We met in 1980. I was twenty, and Chris was twenty-three. I was from California, and he was from the Midwest. We had different family backgrounds. I was in nursing school and living at home. He had been on his own since age eighteen, had a full-time job, and was taking classes at night. He had come alone to California to try to find a new life. Both of us were affected by divorce, and each of us was affected by our family history of alcoholism.

When we first met our relationship was based primarily on physical attraction and a desire to escape the loneliness we both felt. Though we were from different backgrounds, we felt comfortable with each other. I thought his family was warm and close, like the TV family the Waltons (not completely accurate), and he noticed that my family was financially stable. I liked that he came home from work at 3:30 p.m., unlike my father who was often gone and not very available when he was home. My mom had left when I was fifteen.

Chris and I were quickly inseparable. We became lovers and best friends, and moved in together eight months later.

When we met he noticed that I didn't drink much, so he was on his best behavior in that area. He slowly discovered that my drug of choice was food. I was five foot two inches and ninety-eight pounds when we first met. I had lost about thirty pounds just prior to meeting him. I began having trouble maintaining that weight loss and was alternating between anorexia and compulsive overeating. My weight dropped to eighty-five pounds, and then I gained about twenty pounds in two months. I was almost suicidal. He was supportive and told me that he would love me no matter how much I weighed. I loved him even more for that, although I didn't believe him. I felt unlovable.

While we were living together, I noticed that he was a daily drinker, although he did not usually get drunk. I was used to that, as both my parents were daily drinkers as well. He would get drunk a few times a month, but he was kind and gentle and happy, so it did not seem to be a problem. However, after nursing school lectures on alcoholism, I became focused on his drinking and began counting and recording the number and types of his drinks. I even presented him with the written evidence of my concerns. He thanked me politely but did not change his behavior. At the same time I was still struggling with food, weight, body image, self-esteem, and depression.

We decided to get married. I had concerns about his drinking, and I am sure that he had concerns about my weight. I think we both underestimated the power of our addictions. I believed that we had the same disease, just different substances—that we would understand and love each other and that together we could face the world. I decided that we would get help someday if necessary. I knew that he was an intelligent, loving, generous, hard-working person who loved me, and that he would make a great father someday. I added a sentence into our wedding vows about seeking help if necessary—just in case.

We married in 1982, and I became a nurse. Chris did become a great dad, and I tried to be supermom. We had a daughter who was the light of our lives. We both worked hard and bought a new home and lived a nice life.

Our addictive behavior became a bigger problem as time went on. I was constantly on a diet, and my weight was up and down, but always climbing higher. My weight and shame about my body interfered with our intimacy, and I was unable to fully participate in life. In response to our addictive behavior, I became anxious, overly sensitive, untrusting, disrespectful, compulsive, and negative. He began to drink more and to withdraw. He became angry, and I became depressed. My weight became his excuse to drink, and his drinking became my excuse to eat. We both continued to put a lot of effort into being the best parents we could be. We continued to love each other and to have good times too, but our marriage was not healthy. We were both disappointed and hurt. If not for our daughter, our marriage would have ended.

I tried to seek help for both of us in 1990, but Chris was resistant. It had never occurred to me that he would not be ready for help at the same time I was. I had about two years of recovery and had reached a fairly normal weight for a while, but I wanted out of the marriage. It scared me. I could not do that to my daughter. I turned back to food. I relapsed and regained the weight. I became very depressed and almost suicidal again, but now I had a five-year-old daughter who I had to stay alive for. My husband was there for me although I had caused him so much pain.

Ten years passed. In 1999 I was up to 205 pounds, and I was desperate enough to seek help again. I joined two twelve-step programs, one for my food problem and one for my codependency problem. I also began attending church regularly. This time in recovery I learned that I could improve my life without leaving my husband, that with enough support and my higher power's help, I could become healthy physically, emotionally, and spiritually.

I received the gift of clarity regarding my food choices and eating behaviors. I have kept off sixty pounds for ten years now. My food and eating behaviors are not perfect but they are greatly improved. My body is not what I would prefer, but my shame about it is mostly healed. I continue to work for improvement with my thinking, my food, and my body without obsessing and/or strict dieting, which can lead me into relapse. I lead a mostly sane, joyful, and balanced life. I still attend both recovery programs.

I wanted our marriage to work. I did not want to destroy our daughter. I wanted our family to be healed. I decided to select my sponsors, therapists, and program friends from the ranks of married people who were equally committed to their marriages as well. I looked for people who took their marriage vows seriously, and I learned from them. I did not want to buy into the fantasy of finding the perfect man somewhere out there. I believe we are all imperfect, and that there would be problems no matter whom I am married to. I also know that statistically I am likely to pick another person with addiction. I loved my husband and wanted to try to make it together.

I learned how not to suffer the effects of my husband's drinking, and I learned that I was responsible for my own happiness. I learned to focus on all of the good things about him and about my life. After I got into recovery, our marriage improved for a few years. Life was pretty good even though he was still drinking more than I would have preferred.

Then my husband injured his back and developed a prescription drug addiction. Life got crazy, especially after our daughter left for college. He was often driving under the influence and was hospitalized twice for drug overdoses. I would come home and find him sitting in the spa in the dark, barely coherent. I was terrified he would drown, and I was so angry I wanted to drown him myself. He *eventually was spending three hundred to seven hundred dollars a week on medications. I closed all of our joint accounts.*

I was in torment until I decided to do an intervention. It was a difficult and scary decision. I did the intervention for all three of us. I was afraid he would die or kill someone, and I needed to know that I had done every loving and constructive thing I could to help him. I also focused on trying not to control him or enable him in any way. Our daughter, who was eighteen at the time, also participated in the intervention. It was a kind and loving intervention, facilitated by a professional, which included other people from my husband's life to validate our experiences and fears for his life. The secret was out in the open. My husband was angry, but at the same time felt loved and valued by his family and friends. It was only partially successful, but it did set the stage for future recovery. He had another drug overdose seven months later.

Shortly after that, I filed for divorce to protect myself from liability. I insisted my husband leave, and I changed the locks. I told him that he could come back when he had six months of recovery. I had no idea if he could or would get sober, but I had to save myself. I didn't know if I would want him back if he was in recovery, but I was not ready to give up my dream of being a healthy family, and I was not willing to take away all of his hope. I only knew that I could not continue the way things were. It was a God thing. God unexpectedly gave me the words and the power and the strength to do this at the perfect time for both Chris and me.

Chris rented an apartment a mile away. During that time we went to counseling and joined a couples meeting. There were times when we had no contact for weeks and times when we had daily contact. Neither of us dated other people. Sometimes we shared physical intimacy with each other and sometimes we did not. I lived alone for the first time in my life. It was a valuable experience for me.

Chris struggled with recovery for about a year. Sometimes he was in recovery and struggling to stay that way, and sometimes he was lying and trying to convince me I was crazy when I questioned his recovery. I finally cut off contact with him because I felt insane and felt I was about to relapse myself. I was done.

About a month later he was found unresponsive outside his apartment and ended up back in the ER. That was when he finally got into recovery. Six months later he moved back into our home. I was unsure whether that was what I wanted, but decided to stick to our original agreement. It was difficult for the first few years. The couples meetings gave us enough hope to keep trying. At one time I became so angry that I physically attacked him, trying to smash his guitar over his head, then sobbed for hours while he held me.

The couples meetings have been crucial for us. About ten to fifteen couples meet once a week for one hour. We have gone fairly regularly for six years. We are lucky to have a couples meeting that stays positive and focuses on solutions and successes. We are careful not to embarrass each other in front of our group. We are both able to learn more about ourselves and each other and about marriage by listening to the other group members. We gained perspective, hope, and courage, and we lost our shame. We came to see ourselves as survivors and not victims.

We have our ups and downs. We still have normal problems, such as the economy and health issues and being different from each other. We have love and respect for each other and are learning to be better partners to each other. Our twenty-six-year-old daughter is a big part of our lives and loves and admires us both. Chris now has six years of recovery; I have almost eleven years of recovery from compulsive overeating and have been attending a program for codependency for ten years. We just celebrated twenty-nine years of marriage.

I am glad I decided to take care of myself and save myself, and that I invited my husband to join me. If asked, I would advise others to stay safe and leave the results and timing up to God. Trust that life will get better somehow if you make a decision to recover. When you stumble, ask for more help and stay on a healthy path. There are many people to help you, and God is in charge. Don't leave before the miracle happens, and remember that you do not know what your miracle will *look like—it may be different than what you had planned. It might even be better. Miracles do happen when you work for them and are willing to ask God and others for help and follow directions.*

Dean and Annette

Dean has been in recovery for thirty-two years, and Annette for eleven; she writes:

> *We have had many crises in our marriage, and our program has often worked despite our conscious intentions. A little over a year ago Dean suffered a major stroke. His social worker and physical therapist told me that my life would never be the same. The social worker said that I must get into a support group for caregivers immediately. I was in a state of shock because Dean had had none of the warning symptoms for a stroke. He had been physically active, although he had slowed down right before the stroke. He never had high blood pressure or high cholesterol.*
>
> *Suddenly I was faced with once again being a caregiver. I had had fourteen years of caregiving for my mother and father. I was retired and was finally able to enjoy life without being responsible for anyone. I was angry. I complained to anyone and everyone who would listen, both in program and out of program. Finally, in a state of resentment and despair, I called my sponsor who very gently said, "How would you feel if it was you who had the stroke and Dean was resentful and bitter?"*
>
> *That one question turned everything around for me. I began treating Dean as I would wish to be treated (for the most part). Several months later I put a deposit on a trip to Greece and another on a cruise to the Mexican Riviera. I frankly never thought Dean would be alive to go with me. A miracle happened. Dean began getting better. He wanted to live. He joined me in an exercise group, and his whole energy was transformed. We just returned from Greece and Turkey, and Dean is healthy. I am in awe of the power of program, prayer, and sponsors to change my attitude and belief in miracles!*

We have summarized the next two stories, which illustrate how couples have utilized their recovery programs to heal from wounds as deep as those caused by infidelity.

Paul and Mary Alice

Paul has been in recovery since 1980, while Mary Alice has been in recovery from her addictions, including codependency, since October 6, 2004. They met on St. Patrick's Day, got pregnant, and were married the following December of their junior year in college. Their marriage has survived a few critical points, with the first being Paul getting into recovery, then Mary Alice twenty-four years later. They had outside help from a counselor familiar with addiction and all its ramifications. During that time, they also relied heavily on sponsors.

Paul's infidelity took place ten years into the marriage and concurrent with getting into recovery. Mary Alice's happened fourteen years later, and before she got into recovery. Mary Alice discovered that her infidelity was entirely related to anger and resentment, which was fueled by her escalating addiction. She states, "Today we are a different couple in so many ways that it is difficult to imagine connection with our history." She indicates that her sobriety and subsequent recovery from food addiction has changed who she is in a significant way. Mary Alice and Paul also sought help from outside sources to address intimacy issues that was foundational to the level of satisfaction they enjoy today. Her advice: "Get help, be patient, and let go of expectations. What you think it should look like is only a hint of what's to come! Stay connected to your recovery tribe." She also found great value in waiting before making a decision to end the relationship and begin again with a new partner. She adds, "Wait to make this decision until your spiritual condition begins to heal. Your happiness does *not* depend on dumping your significant other. In fact, quite the opposite may be true. It may depend on your commitment to him or her."

Paul and Mary Alice have been married for forty years, and are grateful that they stayed together long enough to enjoy a relationship that is now satisfying for both of them.

Dorothy and Joe

Dorothy and Joe were married in 1956, and both got into recovery in 1971. After being in recovery for ten years, Joe's infidelity threatened to end their life together. At the time, they had already been married twenty-five years and had two children whom they loved dearly. They searched their souls and sought guidance from a higher power to save their marriage. They were able to work their recovery programs in order to recommit to their marriage. They relied heavily on use of sponsorship, meetings, counseling, couples groups, and couples retreats. Thirty years after the crisis, they report being very glad that they stayed together. They are both still in recovery and have been married fifty-five years.

Herb and Mary

Herb and Mary experienced a miracle in their relationship through working their recovery programs, the magic of amends, praying for guidance together, letting go of the results, and patience. Herb writes:

> We got into recovery in our eighteenth year of marriage. It was Mary's idea. Drinking had been an integral part of the lives of our families of origin, our dating, our business activities, and all of our married social life.

> We were clueless that alcohol was at the core of all of our troubles.

> We had read books on marriage, gone to marriage counselors, engaged in individual therapy, went to retreats, went to church, tried Marriage Encounter, and talked incessantly with each other about our relationship. Nothing changed. Actually, it got worse.

> We doubled our effort at all of these activities once we got into recovery. In addition, we went to meetings, we talked with our respective sponsors, and we each worked the steps to the best of our ability. And still nothing changed. Actually, it got even worse.

> At the beginning of my fifth year of recovery, I met a man who shared differently in meetings. He talked about doing the steps out of the Big

Book with the guidance of a "step guide"—doing precisely what the book suggested and having a spiritual awakening. I asked him for help, to guide me through the steps. It took eleven months. I began to have a change in my perception, and therefore, my attitude during the work in the Step Four inventory, specifically the fourth column of the work on resentments—my role. I began to realize I am responsible for my feelings and especially for my behavior, 100 percent.

This allowed me to see and objectively evaluate the harm that I had done as I made my Eighth Step list. The Big Book's suggestion and my guide's experience was that I am powerless to change my past, but I must acknowledge it and change my attitude and actions in the present. And I need power, so I pray.

My step guide and prayer prepared me for the amends process with my wife. How do you repair the damage resulting from eighteen years of addictive drinking, delusional thinking, warped feelings, and mean-spirited, self-centered behavior?

The formula included guidance from experienced people, both program and professional. It included a process of prayer and action. It included a lot of personal commitment and effort. It included an open mind and an open heart to know and to do the right thing, and an interpretation of God's will to the best of each of our abilities. It included a desire for the happiness of the other person.

I made an appointment to meet with my wife to discuss these harms and the amends. As part of the process, I acknowledged that I did not know whether to stay or to leave. She was equally ambivalent about the marriage. I asked if she would be willing to pray with me for guidance and healing on a daily basis. She said she was willing.

Since then, and for three years afterwards, each day we got on our knees, held hands, looked into each other's eyes, and prayed out loud for guidance and healing—a spontaneous prayer from the heart. The first time I prayed; the next day she prayed.

Well, you can't do this and stay mad. Within a week we were conscious that the negative heat between us had diminished. Several weeks later we each made independent decisions to get additional personal help.

When we accepted our powerlessness over our past and the effect on our marriage, but took personal responsibility for the present (our feelings and actions) and sought guidance in prayer and healing through our individual and cooperative actions, a miracle resulted. We cannot get here from there—but here we are!

There is a wonderful alchemy when grace meets willingness and action is taken.

We have been married forty-five years and are really good friends. Our life is not perfect. We have not transcended our humanness. But the word we most often use to describe our personal and our married life is that it flourishes. Yes, flourishes.

She respects me; I cherish her. We have a "competition of generosity."

Bill and Karen

Bill has been in recovery since March 27, 1985, and Karen since July 28, 1990. As of August, 2011, they have been together seventeen years and have been married twelve years. Bill writes:

I had split up with my second wife and two kids at about ten years of recovery and was living in a storeroom over my office. Life was not too bright at the time. My whole world had turned upside down, and I was in a pretty sad state. Karen and I began to see each other and the party began. She had never been married, had lived on her own most of her life, and had a great job making good money. She did not need me; she just wanted me! I had never been with a woman that I could not dominate or control. This was an independent woman who had been around the track a few times and knew what she wanted.

We had a wonderful time together. It was like high school; we couldn't keep our hands off each other. The "Bill relationship workshop" was that for the first couple of years, you don't talk about any heavy stuff, which gives the illusion of intimacy but is just us talking about ourselves again. Just have obsessive sex and spend too much money. Have a good time! It's supposed to be fun, not analytical.

We began to fight over things. Karen wanted to bring me into her world and out of mine. She didn't want my kids or all the guys I sponsored. She wanted to bring me into her isolated life. She was in recovery but had no sponsor and didn't work the steps, just went to meetings. She never shared or took birthdays. People really didn't know who she was.

Karen got a sponsor who made her go to a women's meeting. She was resistant to that, as she didn't like or trust women. She is a survivor, and in her jungle other women were the enemy!

She is now one of the queens of her home group, and it is a source of great comfort and humor in her life. She worked the steps and began to tell her story. She was a very stubborn case who went through countless detox centers. When her blood alcohol level would get too low, she would have seizures. When she began sharing these stories, the women started lining up asking for help. This changed her whole world. She has opened up like a flower in bloom. The change has been truly remarkable.

It was and is important to me to be able to share this life with someone who is on the same spiritual path, someone who has the same enthusiasm for recovery as I do. Not easy to find, and having found it, I truly cherish it. I couldn't go into her world; she had to come into mine. Now it is ours.

We both have sponsors. We have a place to go when there is conflict. Early on there was a lot of conflict, but we made the commitment to stay together and work through it. We meditate together. Our days are full of other people so we are not the center of each other's lives. There is not much time to contemplate the relationship, which to us is simply a subtle form of self-obsession, which is the root of our problem. My happiness is not dependent upon her behavior.

In the past, when working on a relationship, the goal was to get the other person to see the error of her ways and to be more sensitive to my needs. Intimacy is when I am able to feel what the other person is feeling, not to just respond to how her feelings affect me. This requires compassion and the offshoots of compassion, patience and tolerance. I learn this from other people in my life and then bring it home. It is not an intellectual process, it is experiential. Now that I am aware, I need to have a series of experiences that cause me to learn lessons that cause me to grow emotionally. I will not think my way into it. No sudden insight will give me the required experience to grow up emotionally.

The biggest problem I have is not the aspects of my nature that don't work…well, those are obvious. The biggest problem is the parts of me that are completely missing, that were never developed. I am emotionally immature, and I need to grow up. I can't speed that process up, but I can certainly slow it down by picking and choosing what I will and won't do. One of the ways I can slow it down is by "working on the relationship!" If I need to get out of myself, and the relationship is part of me, then the less "working on the relationship" I do, the better.

Today life is truly wonderful. I love my wife more today than I ever have. I am proud of her; I respect her. She is my true soul mate, and she has healed me. She sponsors a lot of women and I a lot of men, so our house is full most of the time. We are more firmly on the spiritual path than ever before, and these people are the messengers. By focusing on them, we see ourselves through their eyes better than we could ever flesh it out on our own.

Through meditation we come to realize that we are not our thinking mind because we can watch our thoughts. We are no longer victims of our minds' thought process. The mind wants to analyze and work on self-centered topics because it is all it thinks about. It takes the past and projects it into the future. There is nothing for it to do in the present moment, so it never goes there. I don't have to change it; it is not an adversarial relationship—I can simply ignore it. It is not me. Whatever it comes up with is not essential.

When I am in that space, I don't react to how Karen feels; I feel how she feels. I am connected to her as I am to all of nature. There is no separation, therefore no conflict. It's not like that all the time, however, but it is a lot of the time.

As long as I don't work on it!

Knowing when to quit

The above stories are great examples of situations in which re-examination and recommitment had positive results, but can or should every marriage be saved? Sometimes we can get good results in marriage from clarifying expectations, specifying behavioral changes required, reaffirming our "must haves" to our partner, and making reasonable compromises. However, sometimes we also need to examine our true motives for staying, beyond the kids. Are our motives driven by fear—of financial insecurity, what others will think, the shame of a broken home, or defining divorce as always being a failure?

We've included so much about staying the course that we are compelled to add that we don't think every relationship should be saved, especially if there is physical or emotional harm to children. Sometimes people may overestimate the value of staying together "for the children." We have a friend we'll call Millie, whose husband was very emotionally abusive to her. She tried repeatedly to work things out with him and gave him serious warnings more than a year in advance of her decision to leave. However, he was uncooperative and there was no change in behavior. Millie's bottom line was the effect on her young girls. If she stayed, she was modeling for them how a woman should be treated, and she did not want them to grow up to have abusive relationships. After her decision to seek a divorce, she was apprehensive about telling the children, but when she did, her eight-year-old "high-fived" her.

The future of each marriage is between the individuals and their own higher powers. In working with others, we should avoid advice-giving as to the future of the relationship. We should just share our own experience, and encourage each individual to seek his or her own solution through working their recovery program. We have found great value in praying and trying to keep an open mind, whether regarding our own relationship or in working with others.

2

COUPLES COMMUNITY

{ *No power, no music* }

By Steve

As we take a first step out of the mire of addiction, dysfunction, isolation, and desperation, we stand at the starting gate of recovery. We then come to understand that lack of power is our dilemma. Despite our best efforts, on our own power we could not create the desired outcome. If lack of power is our dilemma, then it follows that power is the solution. What would I do if I wanted to listen to some music and when I tried to turn on the stereo, nothing happened? Well, I would probably first make sure it was plugged in.

No power, no music. Do we need to understand how electricity works in order to enjoy its benefits? Of course not. However, once we are connected to the power grid, the needed power is there.

The same is true for the power which is available to support our union. We can take advantage of this power, whether we understand it or not. The best way I know to begin to describe the power experienced in community is the following list:

- **Hope**—if others have overcome difficulties, maybe we can, too.

- **Connection through identification**—in sharing our stories, we can relate with the similarities of experiences and emotions.

- **Unity/singleness of purpose**—when we share common challenges, the desire to overcome them, and a common solution, it creates a bond and an opportunity for community.

- **Courage, compassion, and love**—after we hear each other's struggles and suffering, we begin to have empathy and can borrow courage from each other.

- **Truth-telling, healing by simply telling our story**—a place is said to be sacred if it is safe to tell your story there.

- **Humility**—when we allow ourselves to be transparent and begin to own our human shortcomings, it has a humbling effect.

- **Wisdom**—knowing the difference between what we do and do not have power over becomes clearer as we listen to each other.

That's a lot of power!

Angie and I intuitively knew—based on our dismal relationship histories—that we were going to need some help. From the beginning we reached out for support from a couples community that had been meeting for many years. We went to our first couples retreat while we were still dating. We were amazed! Here were healthy role models, the proof that marriages could survive seemingly insurmountable obstacles, such as death of children or infidelity, using spiritual principles. Some of these were marriages of many decades, where the couples had been in active addiction together and gone through the recovery process together. We thought, "These people must really know something about forgiveness." We were openly embraced as newcomers, and we hung on their every word. Hope grew deep within us. If they could do it, maybe we could, too! After all, we were starting out together with a solid recovery background and no baggage with each other.

So often for me, higher power is made of flesh and blood—it talks through other people. I seem to be more willing to seek counsel and take direction from people who have direct experience. Here was a whole community of couples who had not only faced my most primal fears but had worked through them. They were willing to share openly about how their personal defects of character interfered with having the relationships they wanted and how they persevered and did their individual work and couples' work. We received support and inspiration from them to go forward in our relationship.

Couples Meetings
By Angie

Logistics

We have been exposed to a variety of couples meeting processes. Some groups meet weekly in a neutral setting, such as a church, and go out to dinner for fellowship before or after the meeting. The group we attend most regularly meets monthly in someone's home, on a rotating basis. We gather at 6:00 p.m. and have a potluck that begins at 6:30 p.m. The host couple provides the main dish, and others bring whatever they choose.

The meeting begins at 7:30 p.m. and ends at 9:00 p.m. The host couple chooses a topic, and one of the partners begins the meeting by reading the format, opening the sharing, and introducing the topic. We ask that couples pass if they shared the previous month, until after everyone else has had an opportunity to share. Newcomers are encouraged to pass if they do not feel comfortable. People share as a couple, meaning that first one partner talks on the topic, then the other. The "other half" of the host couple closes the meeting.

When we attended our first couples meeting, it was frightening for us. We agreed that we would not talk about an issue in the group if we had not first discussed it with each other—in other words, no "blindsiding" or surprises. We encourage other couples to do the same. In the beginning, we were madly in love, deeply grateful to have found each other, and did not have any problems. I am ashamed to say I think we may have thought we were immune to the challenges faced by other couples. Eventually, we fell off our pink cloud! Having listened to how others overcame difficulties really came in handy when we began to have a few of our own.

Sample Topics

Over the years, we've discussed a variety of subjects. Sometimes a couple chooses a challenge they are currently facing and asks others to share their experience on that topic. I thought it would be helpful to list some examples of topics:

- What I like/admire about you

- I feel loved when…

- How do you handle conflict?

- Trust, how it grows or withers

- Finances

- Communication

- How (and why) do you stay together?

- Overcoming challenges

- Amends

- Working traditions (our common welfare, unity, etc.)

- How we got together/what attracted us in the first place

- What support looks like to me

- The victory of surrender

- What have you done to keep the romance alive?

- Coping with change

- Positive actions that have benefited the relationship

- How we make key decisions as a couple

- How we grow spiritually as a couple

- Laughter/playfulness in our relationship

- Gratitude

More Observed Benefits

We have written about the power in the couples community, along with some of the general benefits derived from that power. The following specific examples occurred in our couples meeting:

• A couple started attending our group in the very early stages of recovery. Although they had been married several years, they reported not feeling like they really knew each other. They did not know if they even liked each other. About a year later, we noticed a dramatic change, and they seemed to truly enjoy being together.

• People have said they are inspired by what others in the group have shared. For example, someone said he was moved to do nice things for his wife after a meeting where the topic was, "I feel loved/supported when…." Someone else reported getting the idea, "I should just try to be nicer to my spouse," as the result of the meeting discussion. Someone else started a gratitude list specifically for the spouse.

• Many of us have noticed positive reinforcement and increased gratitude for our relationships as a direct result of the meetings. It helps us to focus on what is right, conceive constructive plans for enhancement, and appreciate our partners even more.

There is just something magical about sharing this process with other couples. The open dialog gives us an opportunity to get ideas and "try on" approaches. It is also valuable to clarify or eliminate undesirable practices. It is not a "one size fits all" thing. For example, we have indicated how well our plan of separate finances works for us. Several years ago there was a highly respected couple in our group whom some might look up to as "gurus." They moved away shortly after we started in the group. In one meeting someone shared about how the "guru couple" always strongly advocated pooling all of your money into one pot. After my initial inward gasp I thought, "Well, thank God they left town!" We think it is so important for each couple to determine, through communication, what works best for them.

The real miracle is that, gradually, our liabilities have been transformed into assets. We have seen how our experience can help others, especially those new in recovery. What a joy to feel that our past pain and suffering has been transformed into a gift that can possibly benefit someone else.

Couples Retreats

We have written about how we were inspired when we attended our first couples retreat while we were dating. Here we will talk about those retreats in more detail. Although on occasion we go to other retreats, our annual "commitment" retreat is on Valentine's weekend.

By the way, it is our understanding that the concept of couples retreats and meetings was heavily influenced by Dr. Paul and Max O. Dr. Paul is the author of *There's More to Quitting Drinking than Quitting Drinking,* Sabrina Publishing, 1995. His story, initially titled "Doctor, Alcoholic, Addict," appears in the third edition of the book *Alcoholics Anonymous*, pages 439 – 452, and reappears in the fourth edition as "Acceptance Was the Answer," pages 407 – 420. He is well known in twelve-step fellowships as the author of an often quoted passage regarding acceptance. Dr. Paul was very interested in continuously improving his relationship with his wife, Max. There is, in fact, an annual retreat entitled the "Dr. Paul and Max O Couples Communication Workshop" in Arrowhead, California. Dr. Paul and Max are now deceased, but they have passed on their legacy to those of us who are privileged to participate and be present to inspire those who will follow us. The workshop format is somewhat similar to that described below for the Valentine Retreat.

We never have to wonder about what to do for Valentine's Day, as we have a gratifying way to acknowledge our love. The retreat begins on Friday night; we have dinner followed by an opening meeting. The coordinator welcomes everyone, makes relevant announcements, and introduces the weekend's leaders. Those leaders have been chosen in advance, at a gathering in September or October. They are always people "from within," who have been attending the retreat and are actively involved in recovery program(s). This practice, incidentally, has created a special bond among the couples and a real feeling of cohesiveness, especially among the many former leaders. Several years ago (long before "our time"), they had brought in "professionals" or "celebrities" from outside the community, and the results were less than favorable. The retreats have been as large as sixty couples, but more often have averaged forty or fewer.

On Friday evening, the lead couple speaks, telling the story of their recovery process, especially as it relates to their relationship with their partner. On Saturday morning after breakfast, we begin break-out sessions, with topics that have been chosen in advance by the leaders. These break-out sessions usually consist of 5 – 8 couples, and are conducted much like the couples meetings we have described, with each couple sharing their experience regarding the topic. After dinner, we have a meeting with the entire group and celebrate recent recovery anniversaries. Next comes the ice cream social, followed by an optional 10:00 p.m. meeting called "Pillow Talk." Sunday morning is the closing meeting, again with the whole group.

More about "Pillow Talk"

"Pillow Talk" was initially started at one of the earlier retreats as a safe meeting to address the topic of sex (that's right, we don't actually talk about bed linens). It had been led by the same couple for several years (again, since way before "our time"). A few years ago they wanted us to take over that service, so we have also led that meeting a few times. Leaders merely set the tone, share their experience openly and honestly, and create a safe atmosphere for others to do likewise. This can be a delicate topic, and one not often discussed in meetings. It is important to not "overshare," as it is not a "how to" meeting, but usually more about intimacy and keeping physical affection alive in the relationship.

At our tenth annual Valentine Retreat, we had an interesting experience. The schedule showed the original couple as leading "Pillow

Talk." We were glad, and thought we would not even go to the meeting, as we would just as soon read and go to bed early. However, the other couple urged us to lead, as they really did want to permanently pass on the responsibility. We agreed, as a matter of service, certainly not that we thought we would get anything out of it ourselves.

It was a small but powerful meeting from which we both benefited. I became aware of some changes that had occurred in my own attitude. For example, my baggage had included being in long-term relationships where my partner was not interested in having sex with me. This had been painful, and I had experienced a great deal of rejection, especially when there was infidelity by my partner. I had also previously equated sex with love. In addition, early in our marriage, it was difficult for me to initiate sex because of my fear of rejection. I also experienced wondering whether Steve was still attracted to me. A lot of this occurred in the adjustment from the early stages of extreme lust to the daily routines of living together. Over time, these feelings had pretty much disappeared, and I had become very comfortable. I realized that the decisions to make love had come to feel much more mutual to me, rather than being initiated by one partner, and that I did not feel upset if Steve wanted to put it off for another time. It was not until I listened to other people that I realized that I had experienced this transformation.

For Steve, a major benefit is not living in the extremes that he described in previous chapters. Through identification, we had both experienced even more gratitude for the state of our marriage. The miracle is that we have balance, contentment, and are able to enjoy a healthy sex life as well as relationship.

The theme seemed to be "the joy of cuddling." We had a long discussion on the way home about the subtopics that emerged, as well as some that would bear further exploration, such as

• Equating sex with love (e.g., do you still love me if we are not having sex as often?), concluding that your partner no longer finds you attractive.

- Planning vs. spontaneity—is it really "unromantic" to plan some of our encounters?

- Do we have to be aroused to begin? Stepping into closeness and trusting that arousal will happen (letting it be okay if it doesn't sometimes).

- Is a sense of humor welcome in the bedroom?

- Vulnerability of initiating, when differing needs do not mean rejection.

- The relationship between sex and intimacy.

- Using sex as a weapon (e.g., withholding).

- Different strokes, stretching sexual boundaries.

- Sacred trust (guarding or rebuilding).

- Adapting to changes that happen with age and relationship stages.

- How does your sex life survive while dealing with challenges, such as raising children, managing households, jobs, or families?

- What happens when the last time we had sex gets further and further away?

- Compromise of desire discrepancies. When not having sex seems easier than trying to have sex.

- Making it a priority.

- Are there unresolved issues standing in the way of a healthy sex life?

More Topics

To assist those who might be thinking of initiating a couples retreat, we are including a few additional topics from previous retreats:

- Shared values.

- Keeping it simple.

- Communication breakdown.

- Hostage or helpmate.

- Balancing separation and togetherness.

- Keeping a higher power in the middle of our relationship.

- Seeing our relationship as half-full, not half-empty.

- Courtesy—keeping our love fresh.

- Intimacy.

- Do you want to be right or loved?

- What has changed in you because of your relationship?

- Are you fighting your partner's battles?

- The victory of surrender.

- How have you been able to say, "Whose quirk is it anyway?"

- How we practice forgiveness.

- Keeping our love fun.

What the Future Holds: A Growing Movement

The Valentine's Retreat has been coordinated by a very dynamic and dedicated couple who have kept it going all these years. The Arrowhead Retreat has been continued by another dedicated couple for as far back as we can remember. Numerous couples have benefited immeasurably, and many have indicated that these retreats have actually saved their marriages. We have witnessed miracles in relationships, where a couple was on the brink of divorce one year and happily recommitted the next. We hope there will always be people who are willing to continue to carry the torch to keep these retreats going and growing. People fly from all over the country to attend these retreats. It is so wonderful to reconnect with people for whom you feel such fondness, yet sometimes only get to see once or twice a year. One participant described it as being "like a family reunion, but one you look forward to." Furthermore, while we truly cherish our weekend retreats, a similar process could occur as a "one-day retreat" or workshop with leaders and break-out groups. This would be relatively inexpensive and logistically easy, as the sessions could be conducted in one day at any number of venues, including churches with good meeting spaces. There are many of us who would love to see "self-help" couples retreats, workshops, and meetings springing up throughout the country, and we would be happy to provide mentoring to help in that endeavor.

SUMMARY

In summary, our experience as single people taught us to

- Be willing to be alone, and to say no to what we did not want.

- Seek spiritual growth by working our recovery programs (which ultimately helped us to feel worthy of a healthy relationship and to overcome fear).

- Be self-supporting.

- Envision the qualities we wanted in a partner.

- Become the partners we wanted to be, nourishing in ourselves the qualities we desired in a mate.

- Seek guidance both from a higher power and from mentors.

- Discover ourselves, what is really important, our core values.

- Communicate our "must haves" and "deal breakers" with each other while dating, and before making a long-term commitment.

Then, as a committed couple, we have benefited from

- Learning to recognize our own negative moods and tendencies in order to avoid blaming them on our partner.

- Weekly inventory meetings.

- Continuously working on improving our communication skills, for example
    - Reiterating what we think we heard.
    - Rating the importance of a want or need on a scale from one to ten.

- Trading annual "what I like about you" lists.

- Praying and meditating together, which can be as simple as
    - A few words of gratitude before a meal.
    - A prayer to turn our will and lives over to our higher power, or to remove our character defects, especially during stressful times or before a discussion of an emotionally-charged issue.

- Keeping a marriage journal.

- Becoming aware of our own unconscious and often unrealistic expectations.

- "Hanging in" when the going gets rough, and recommitting. (One of our mentors once said, "Marriage is like a long railroad track; sometimes you hit a bad stretch, but if you stay on the track it gets good again.")

- Admitting when we are wrong and making prompt amends; receiving amends from each other with forgiveness and grace.

- Being open to trying new things.

- Getting "away from it all" together.

- Taking time for our individual interests, which also makes us appreciate each other more.

- Working on expressing gratitude frequently, especially for the little things we do for each other that might be taken for granted.

- Establishing new traditions.

- Attending couples meetings and retreats, which heighten our appreciation of each other.

- Respecting each other's recovery programs, continuing to work our own programs, and being of service to others.

In wrapping up, we thought we should add something about keeping romance alive. We realize we know only a little, especially compared to some who have been married much longer. We had already caught ourselves falling into some pretty unromantic habits, like discussing plumbing or household chores prior to planning to engage in lovemaking (embarrassing but true). Fortunately, we became aware of our "not good foreplay" activities and have made efforts to change. We can only imagine how challenging it must be for couples with additional pressures, such as raising children. For some people, having a specific "date night" has been beneficial. Although our "renewal" times are often deliberate, they are usually more oriented toward special events or retreats. We know we will never return to that initial euphoric state of effortlessly passionate romance (where for a time Steve even enjoyed Angie's singing). However, we now share a much deeper connection and union. We are best friends, with a contented and loving partnership.

Probably every couple has their own ways of expressing affection. We enjoy giving each other forehead kisses, which are truly wonderful because they mean that someone loves you and doesn't want anything from you. One thing we have particularly cherished is a custom CD that we made around the time of our engagement. That music, which we were listening to while we were falling in love, can reawaken the profound joy of having found each other.

In attempting to write about romance, we realized that most of this book is really about building the foundation we need to keep romance alive. For example, how romantic can we feel when we are resentful or not communicating in a healthy way? The bottom line is that by continuing to grow and practice spiritual principles, we have an opportunity to enjoy not only romance but true, lasting love and partnership.

APPENDIX I

Sample Couples Meeting Format

Start the meeting with the Serenity Prayer:

> *God, grant us the serenity*
> *to accept the things we cannot change,*
> *the courage to change the things we can,*
> *and the wisdom to know the difference.*

One member of the host couple leads the meeting, opening with the following statement:

> *We are a group of couples who have come together for the*
> *purpose of supporting each other in our relationships. We do this*
> *by use of the spiritual principles of the twelve-step programs.*
> *We share our experience, strength, and hope with each other*
> *in a kind and caring way.*
>
> *We regard our commitments respectfully and seriously, learning*
> *and trying constantly to "keep our side of the street clean."*
>
> *We ask God as we understand God to help us in this*
> *"one day at a time."*
>
> *We ask that couples who shared the previous month pass*
> *unless everyone has already had an opportunity to share.*
> *Anyone (such as newcomers to the group) not comfortable*
> *with sharing may also pass.*

Host couple chooses a topic and one partner starts the sharing. The "other half" of the host couple closes the sharing.

At the end of the sharing, plan for next month's meeting location.

Choose someone to close out the meeting with the prayer of their choice.

Also Available from Central Recovery Press

www.centralrecoverypress.com

BEHAVIORAL HEALTH

Disentangle: When You've Lost Your Self in Someone Else
Nancy L. Johnston, MS, LPC, LSATP • $15.95 US
ISBN-13: 978-1-936290-03-1

From Heartbreak to Heart's Desire: Developing a Healthy GPS (Guy Picking System)
Dawn Maslar, MS • $14.95 US • ISBN-13: 978-0-9818482-6-6

INSPIRATIONAL

The Truth Begins with You: Reflections to Heal Your Spirit
Claudia Black, PhD • $17.95 US • ISBN-13: 978-1-936290-61-1

Above and Beyond: 365 Meditations for Transcending Chronic Pain and Illness
J.S. Dorian • $15.95 US • ISBN-13: 978-1-936290-66-6

Guide Me in My Recovery: Prayers for Times of Joy and Times of Trial
Rev. John T. Farrell, PhD • $12.95 US • ISBN-13: 978-1-936290-00-0

Special hardcover gift edition
$19.95 US • ISBN-13: 978-1-936290-02-4

The Soul Workout: Getting and Staying Spiritually Fit
Helen H. Moore • $12.95 US • ISBN-13: 978-0-9799869-8-7

Tails of Recovery: Addicts and the Pets That Love Them
Nancy A. Schenck • $19.95 US • ISBN-13: 978-0-9799869-6-3

Of Character: Building Assets in Recovery
Denise D. Crosson, PhD • $12.95 US • ISBN-13: 978-0-9799869-2-5

MEMOIRS

Leave the Light On: A Memoir of Recovery and Self-Discovery
Jennifer Storm • $14.95 US • ISBN-13: 978-0-9818482-2-8

The Mindful Addict: A Memoir of the Awakening of a Spirit
Tom Catton • $18.95 US • ISBN-13: 978-0-9818482-7-3

Becoming Normal: An Ever-Changing Perspective
Mark Edick • $14.95 US • ISBN-13: 978-0-9818482-1-1

Dopefiend: A Father's Journey from Addiction to Redemption
Tim Elhajj • $16.95 US • ISBN 13: 978-1-936290-63-5